T0368154

BROKEN *But* HEALING

BELLA ST. PATRICK
and ARISTA

BALBOA.PRESS
A DIVISION OF HAY HOUSE

Balboa Press books may be ordered through booksellers or by contacting:

Balboa Press
A Division of Hay House
1663 Liberty Drive
Bloomington, IN 47403
www.balboapress.com
844-682-1282

Print information available on the last page.

ISBN: 979-8-7652-5552-0 (sc)
ISBN: 979-8-7652-5553-7 (hc)
ISBN: 979-8-7652-5551-3 (e)

Library of Congress Control Number: 2024919271

Balboa Press rev. date: 12/05/2024

Contents

Chapter 1 "My Rock and My Roots" 1
Chapter 2 Welcome to the World! ~ "Roses and Thorns" 11
Chapter 3 Bella Blooms ~ in Bloomington, Indiana 20
Chapter 4 School Daze ~ "A Rebel with a Cause" 31
Chapter 5 To Catch a Thief & Mad Dog ~ "...Love is in the Air" 44
Chapter 6 Back to Mayberry ~ The Good, the Bad and.......... 54
Chapter 7 ...and The Ugly... ~ "Kevin and *Lemon Drops*" 68
Chapter 8 ...The Loss of "My Rock" ~ "Love Lands Me in Hell" 87
Chapter 9 From *Deep Hell*...I Emerge ~ "A House is not a Home" 105
Chapter 10 "Revelation – Rehab" ~ Deep Hell to SHELTER.... 118
Chapter 11 "Rising from The Abyss ~ Through the Open Door" 127
Chapter 12 The Sun Shines Through ~ "Transformation—Resolutions" 142
Chapter 13 "How Does My Garden Grow?" ~ "HOME" 168

Resources Page 175
Author Bios 177

A Story of Life

Love

Compassion

Courage

Forgiveness

The Journey "Home"

to

Your "True Self"

This book is dedicated:

To All

My Sisters and Brothers

who are enduring harm and pain

So, you know 'You are not alone'

We are all here with you

Reach out!

Life and Love

Your Hope & Dreams

Await you!

Chapter 1

"My Rock and My Roots"

My story begins by introducing "The Rock" of our family, my *Granny*. She laid the foundation for everything I am. If it weren't for her being the major influence in my life, I may not even be here to tell my story. My grandmother was born Angela Jenkins on June 11, 1931 in South Orange, New Jersey, to her mother, Lucille Jenkins. (Nothing is known about Granny's father. It was never mentioned, nor did she want it mentioned. She was a survivor from day one and walked on her own two legs, never looking back.) Ironically, Granny was born in the era known as *The Silent Generation*. Her silence was her quiet strength; you could sense it when she spoke, and you listened because you knew what she had to say was important.

My Grandmother Angela had 6 sisters and 2 brothers...although it could have been up to 10 siblings, and I know one of her sisters, Evelyn died in a fire. That must have been rough going for such a big family; the Great Depression didn't end till 1939, and then you had Hitler and World War II right on its heels. Granny would reminisce how she picked tomatoes, pulled corn, and picked crabs as a child during the post-Depression era. She was educated in the Bloomington, Indiana, school system and went all the way through high school there.

From what I can remember, Granny and her mother, Lucille

Jenkins, had a good relationship; she talked about her mom, and I know she loved her. I didn't get to know my great-grandmother Lucille that well. I was only seven years old when she died. Still, I do remember very well *the reason why* my mom Bridgette and I ended up going to my great-grandmother's funeral—which we had not planned to attend. But because of some crazy incident I concocted, we would suddenly make an appearance there. Granny had already flown home to South Orange, New Jersey for her mother's funeral, leaving just me and my mother in Granny's house, and my mother was about 9 months pregnant with my brother Brandon.

For whatever reason, that day—at 7 years old—I decided to play the devil. While mom was in my grandmother's room enjoying some quiet time—reading a book, drinking some iced tea, and watching TV—I was searching for some mischief and found it in a pack of matches. I said to myself, "Let me see how this works," and I struck, and struck, and struck them until the matches caught on fire. I was in the kitchen, and suddenly seeing the lit sticks in my hand, I panicked and threw the matches underneath the table 'cuz *now* I really got scared. Then, I ran back into Granny's room and sat next to my mother, but soon made a quick decision—to hide underneath the bed—would it be safer there?? From the house blowing up?? My mother now distracted by my behavior, turned to me, "Bella, what's wrong?" I answered innocently, "Oh, nothin'... -Bella, *what's wrong?"* Her tone changed...she knew something was wrong.

She followed my steps back into the kitchen and as I was peeking from under the bed, I heard a ruckus, as Bridgette quickly took steps to put out the fire. The sky didn't fall, she didn't scream or scold me but the silence was 'deafening' that night. The next thing I knew, the next morning, my mother and I were on a plane to New Jersey to attend my great-grandmother Lucille's funeral. Honestly, I think my mother was scared to be in the house with me by herself! ...And she wasn't taking any chances. – That day, *I was terrible.*

One thing I did learn about my great-grandmother was that Granny, growing up under her mother's guidance, was introduced to the merciful love of Jesus Christ at First Baptist Church of Unionville, in Bloomington, Indiana. This had a profound influence on Granny and served her well throughout her life. She gained and lived with a deep awareness of God's many blessings. This was the essential core of Granny's strength on which she built her own house to weather all the challenges that she and her family would face. Later, when my brothers and I came along, Granny would instill the Bible and its teachings in us and make the Church a major part of our lives.

My Granny Angela married Kenneth Williams Jr. when they were very young. My grandfather was born on February 19, 1929, to Kenneth Williams, Sr. and Virginia Turner who were sharecroppers. My Grandfather Kenneth was a very handsome man, well-built, 5' 11," with chocolate complexion. We all called him Pop Pop; Kenneth Jr. joined the Navy in 1947 and went out to sea on the USS Hank and the USS New Jersey Battleships. After finishing his tour, he married Granny and they had three daughters: Jacqueline, Joan, and Bridgette. Bridgette was the youngest and is my mom.

Aunt Jacqueline was the oldest and is my Godmother. She was drop-dead gorgeous and looked just like a movie star. She stood 5 '5", weighed about 135 pounds, and had flawless skin and an exquisite hazelnut complexion. When she walked, she had this bouncy, shoulder-length hair that was always blowing in the wind. In fact, I recall telling my Aunt Jacqueline that she reminded me of B. Smith (the restaurateur/model) because they looked so much alike and were both such classy, elegant women. I always looked up to my Aunt Jacqueline from the time she became a flight attendant in 1981 and relocated to St. Louis, Missouri.

I'll never forget when she moved to St. Louis and we visited her there. Aunt Jacqueline lived in this fabulous apartment with floor-to-ceiling windows that wrapped around so you could see a view of the city wherever you looked. It was like stepping onto a Hollywood movie set. I was amazed - it reminded me of the rich people I saw on television.

Aunt Jacqueline passed away on March 14, 2016, due to a severe asthma attack. As a flight attendant, Jacqueline was a part of the Class Action Lawsuit back in the 1990s brought on by American

Airlines Employees who sued their company for hazardous working conditions. Thousands of employees became sick from the chemicals used to clean the planes' interiors which were not allowed to dry properly. This resulted in thousands of people having breathing problems and asthma-related issues. Aunt Jacqueline never married or had children but her independence and her successful career were always an inspiration to me and added to my Granny's love for traveling.

My Aunt Joan, the middle daughter, is also a stunner and she is very outgoing. Joan is taller at 5'8", medium build, and weighs about 150 pounds. She is light-skinned, highly intelligent, and *cool as shit*. She always wears the latest fashions and she was the first person I knew who had a fur coat. Aunt Joan is very into her African American culture; she always had engaging African sculptures and paintings displayed in her home since I was little. Aunt Joan had one child, Marcus King Jr., born on February 14, 1972. Her husband at the time was Marcus King Sr. My cousin Marcus and I were close all through childhood and I always felt a special closeness to my Aunt Joan, who is still with us.

Bridgette is the youngest of Granny's daughters and is my mom. She inherited her sisters' good looks. My mother Bridgette Williams Thomas is a beautiful woman. At 5'6" and 150 pounds, she is a perfect size 8 with caramel-colored, flawless skin. Long, beautiful black, shoulder-length hair and pretty brown eyes completed the picture. My mother had a style of her own. Her makeup was always done to perfection and on point. She had three children, myself Bella St. Patrick, and then my brother, Brandon Simmons, followed by the youngest Jayden Thomas...yes, we all had different last names which will be explained later.

When my grandparents Pop Pop and Granny married, I'm not sure they even had a home of their own because they were just teenagers—probably about 16 or so as they were born in 1931 and 1929—and Granny was about 17 or 18 when she had her 3rd child. Things started going south shortly after that and they divorced. My grandmother showed her true colors early—if it's not working, it's not working and she divorced Kenneth Williams Jr. and had no problem moving on.

After their divorce, Granny relocated to Philadelphia, Pennsylvania where she met and married Nigel Collins. Reverend Collins was a minister and served in the Air Force. As Nigel was in the military, he and my grandmother traveled to many different states and places where he was stationed. Twenty years later, my step-grandfather retired in Indiana and that's how my family ended up being raised in Bloomington, Indiana.

Together my grandmother and Reverend Collins founded the First Baptist Church of Unionville, in Bloomington, Indiana. At Church, my grandmother taught Sunday School, sang in the choir, and was a member of the Minister's Wives Alliance. Our family church was a lovely, long brown-brick building, medium in size with a wonderful interior. It was always filled with love, laughter, and joyous singing. I loved going to Church every Sunday. Granny and Reverend Collins were happily married until his untimely death in 1973 from a sudden cardiac problem. The Reverend also owned property—4 or 5 homes—so between their active community work at the Church and his real estate, their cup runneth over. Once Nigel my step-grandfather died, my mother told me about the biggest home of their properties but I never got to live in that particular house. Following Granny's husband's death, it was too much for my grandmother to take care of all the rental properties. Maybe she didn't have the real estate business sense then—so she sold all of them, except the one we lived in which was a smaller house.

What happened to my grandfather Pop Pop after Granny divorced him? He was about 17 then and he went into the Navy. When he came out of the service, he worked as a Corrections Officer at the local prison for a few years and then got remarried to a woman named Wanda Nichols. They had five children together, 2 boys and 3 girls, and that's when Pop Pop bought his first truck and started the crabbing business. One guy brought a bushel of crabs to him and he bought them; then, he started buying more and more, and finally, he hit upon the idea and said, "Wait, wait a minute. I can do something with this," and he expanded from one truck and a bushel of crabs to an entire business. He had a fleet of Mercedes trucks, with 10-20 trucks delivering crabs to New York and New Jersey nightly.

Though my grandfather, Kenneth Williams, Jr., grew up dirt poor—the offspring of sharecroppers—he turned out to be a very enterprising businessman and eventually became a self-made millionaire. -Pop Pop created a successful crabbing business. He started his own wholesale/retail seafood establishment named, KW's Seafood Shack, located in South Orange, New Jersey. The famous local business shipped crabs as far as Europe and Japan for nearly 25 years before my grandfather retired in 1993. Pop Pop passed away on May 08, 2005.

Pop Pop was a millionaire on paper all day long. He really did great for himself. After he passed, I called the local newspaper The News-Gazette and asked them to write an article about his life. I felt he deserved it, which they did with no hesitation; I really appreciated it. However, and this is a big *however,* my grandfather was a millionaire with "no class." He still hung out with the same poor people he grew up with and worked with. He never ventured out to associate with like-minded businessmen as he was, nor did he ever desire to travel and see the world. Yes, he had plenty of cash, but he didn't know what to do with all that money. Granny told me years ago, "Money can't buy you class." If Granny had been with him when he became successful, she would have introduced him to the finer things in life. His 2nd wife Wanda never cared if they left South Orange, New Jersey, just as long as they bought a new car ever so often, had clothes, and had a home—that was enough. Pop Pop kept adding on to his house, so he had the biggest house in the area.

He also had two decrepit trailers right across the street, what a view! Your property value goes down tremendously when you have run-down shanties in the same zip code. The man was so scared someone was going to steal from him, he didn't want to build a home too far away from his business so he had cameras installed, and at night he would look out from his bed at the cameras monitoring his property. That way he could make damn sure no one was breaking in.

Anyone who had class would have moved into a great neighborhood and would have enjoyed life. You don't have a house with cameras and security systems and when you open the window, someone's pissing outside their trailer.

So, although my grandfather Pop Pop had become a millionaire, my grandmother had something you cannot buy – "Class." Even though Granny grew up in hard times—the post-Depression era—I believe Granny was just born with class. She knew early on that she wanted something out of life and also knew she wasn't going to take being abused by any man, including a husband. My grandmother had great insight, even as a young woman (a teenager, no less). Granny knew her worth and that's why she got out of Indiana real quick, ending one chapter and starting a new one—never looking back.

My grandmother was a very beautiful, light-skinned woman with reddish auburn hair that shimmered in the sun. She was 5'5" tall and weighed about 165 pounds—a perfect size 12—a small waist with hips and ass for days. Even with her long skirts and dresses, Granny could not hide her voluptuous shape! She always dressed for success with matching purses, hats, and shoes, and of course her diamond rings and earrings; she loved her beautiful jewelry. Her favorite color was yellow, and although she loved wearing all the bright vibrant colors of the rainbow, Granny always walked with confidence and class. When she entered a room she definitely stood out, and when she spoke, you automatically knew she was intelligent, sophisticated, and had traveled the world.-

My grandmother had a beautiful two-story, 4 bedroom, 2 ½ bath Colonial style home with a full basement and huge kitchen. It had a large garden in the backyard, filled with tomatoes, cucumber, and okra. Fresh vegetables were a must in her house. Her home was the heart, where the entire family would come and enjoy the holidays. It wasn't *really a mansion* but that's what it was in my eyes.

And the aromas that came from her kitchen were so tantalizing; everyone gathered there. I can still smell and taste all the distinct flavors. One of Granny's greatest loves was cooking in her huge kitchen for the entire family. We were lucky kids and feasted on the likes of barbecue ribs, fried pork chops, crab cakes, fried chicken, homemade macaroni and cheese, chitlins, pigs' feet, and plenty of fresh vegetables—collard greens, mustard, and turnip greens, and sweet potatoes.

She also made lots of homemade desserts; the most popular were her mouth-watering pound cakes and sweet potato pies. People raved about them. Yes, Granny really enjoyed cooking, period; and she loved making her own creations, like when she would put some mixture together and make hot water cornbread right in the frying pan. We truly enjoyed our big family holiday meals when all my aunts, uncles, and cousins would gather at. Granny's house: it was filled with laughter, happiness, and joy, especially during the holidays. We would sit in the kitchen while Granny was cooking and my aunts were cooking right alongside her, but not me. Sorry, it just wasn't my thing—there were enough cooks in the kitchen—ain't no need me being there too. As long as I was eating, that's all that mattered to me!

Lucky for my generation, my baby brother Jayden took Granny's cooking gene. After she passed, he pretty much took over cooking everything because my old aunts weren't doing a whole bunch of cooking then, and you already know I wasn't interested—not in the least.

As a young kid, I recall I would sit on my mom's lap while she, Granny, and my aunts would play pinochle and spades, listening to music playing in the background like the Gapband's "Early in the Morning" and Evelyn Champagne King's "Love Come Down" all the while enjoying my mom's homemade iced tea. My mother would be smoking her Benson and Hedges' cigarettes; my Aunt Joan smoked Virginia Slims and Aunt Jacqueline smoked little cigarettes called Capris. I remember when I was about nine, I would ride my bike to the store for my mom with money and a note to buy her cigarettes.

Granny was very active and had many interests. She loved bowling, reading, movies, cooking, crocheting, and traveling. She traveled extensively—all over the world. Among the favorite countries she visited were Jerusalem, Greece, Hawaii, Guam, Mexico, Venezuela, and England. She traveled throughout the United States and went on numerous cruises as well. Besides her luscious pound cakes, she was known throughout the community for her beautiful, crocheted Afghans.

I admire my grandmother so much. She was only 18 when she saw the writing on the wall, and she wasn't about to put up with abuse. Instinctively, she knew her worth. Granny didn't procrastinate but got a divorce and set forth on a better path for herself and her daughters in Philadelphia. And when her second husband Reverend Collins passed suddenly in 1973—whom she loved and enjoyed 20 happy years of married life with—she became a widow at 40. But that didn't cause her to withdraw into grief, she kept right on living and making a difference in the Church and her community. Granny had been a First Lady until her husband the Reverend Collins passed away. But years later when she relocated back to New Jersey, she rejoined her hometown church and continued her Christian life. There, my grandmother served as Vice-President of the Senior Choir, President of the United Methodist Women, and Lay Leader.

In New Jersey, I always have memories of Granny reading her bible at home. She would teach us bible verses and always taught us to be kind and treat people with respect. She was definitely a class act; I think that's one of the reasons why I miss her so much.

My grandmother retired from the University of Illinois, where she worked as an Executive Assistant in the College of Agriculture Department. When she moved back home to New Jersey, she lived with her daughter Bridgette and son-in-law Robert Thomas until her passing on October 26, 2008.

I was fortunate to spend a great part of my life with Granny, going back and forth from New Jersey to Indiana. She had the most profound effect on me that in many ways shaped my entire life. – I looked up to my grandmother. She was beautiful, stylish and sophisticated, financially stable and a homeowner.

I can remember one very special thing my grandmother taught us. Maybe I was about 18, and she sat down and talked to me, my two brothers, and my cousin Marcus (Aunt Joan's son), and she gave us a serious lesson about 'our credit.' She explained to us how it worked—how you can mess up your credit, but that it's something you can always rebuild, but you can never have as much money as you can have credit. She'd say, "You can have $10,000 in the bank but you might have $100,000 worth of credit, so *never* mess up your credit." Most African American families I personally know are never educated about 'credit.'

So, I took up the quest—anybody I came in contact with—be it working at the doctor's office or the jail, I tell them, "Look, I would teach a class free to let you know about the importance of your credit." - When I moved to New Jersey, I have friends I met whose family members would put the electric bills in their kids' names when they were 5 and 6 years old. So, before they were even 18 their credit was screwed. It's sad. Luckily, I came from a different background; that's one of the number one things my Granny taught us. You notice, I say *"my Granny taught us."* Now we had my mother, my Aunts, Joan, and Jacqueline—and Jacqueline was not a mom—so it should have been up to Bridgette (my mother) to teach us but 'really,' it was *"Granny who taught us everything."*

In this whole big family, it was Granny who was the Queen of Wisdom, the Matriarch, and the Mother of All. And as you see in this chapter on my "Roots," there is not much mention of 'fathers;' that's because they weren't there. They sired us and left. But we all felt so loved and cared for it didn't matter. Granny was at the helm, holding everything together.

Honestly, I never really missed having a father because my grandmother replaced my father. My Granny was both Mother and Father to all of us. My grandmother was "My Rock and My Roots," and I am forever grateful. - I miss and revere her every day of my life.

Chapter 2

Welcome to the World! "Roses and Thorns"

On June 10th, 1973, a beautiful, sweet baby girl was born onto the Earth. That would be 'me,' and I weighed in at only 5 lbs. The nurse told my mother I was going to be petite—a little one. I was named Bella St. Patrick—'Bella' meaning *beautiful*, and 'St. Patrick' usually is coupled with the *'lucky shamrock'*...of which I would need plenty because my path in life would be filled with many "Roses and Thorns." This is how my story began, a little rocky at the beginning but not to worry, I came in with a strong backbone and plenty of love thanks to "My Rock"—*Granny*— whom you just learned about, and there will be plenty of memorable Roses too.

My mother, Bridgette Williams, married my father, Michael Daniel St. Patrick and they had me their one and only child together. Neither the marriage nor my father's presence in my life would last long—as my parents separated shortly after I was born and then divorced. I would never meet the man who was my father until I was 23 years old. My mother never spoke about my father. -If you remember, the word *father* was never spoken in our home...because they were never there or not for long.

When I was 6 months old, my Grandfather Collins was holding me in his arms when he had a sudden heart attack and died, so I never got to know my step-grandfather, Granny's second husband. I wish I would have; he sounds like a very nice man. He was a minister, Reverend Nigel Collins, and Granny's "great love" so he must have treated her well…unlike her first husband—Kenneth Williams, Jr. (Pop Pop, my real grandpa)—whom she divorced lickety-split at 23 years old. Even as a teenager, Granny was already a Tower of Strength—"You put your hands on me *just once* and I'm outa here so fast, you won't see my shadow." But that didn't happen with her 2nd husband, Nigel. He was an Air Force man and they traveled all over the country, wherever his military career took him. He was the true love of her life.

I remember a story Granny told me that happened when she and Nigel were a young married couple. This time they were living in one of the southern states, maybe Mississippi. One day husband and wife were leisurely driving to a store in the country and having arrived, they opened the car doors and started walking toward the market when suddenly their eyes riveted on a sign which read, "Whites Only." The letters were clear and bold, no mistaking the warning. Suddenly, the door flew open and they could see 3 or 4 white men emerge, walking towards them at a fast pace. Granny and her husband knew they weren't coming to welcome them. They high tailed it back to their car, quickly locked the car doors, and sped off as fast as they could. Granny said, "I don't know what would have happened to us if Nigel and I had continued into the store." That is one of the few stories Granny ever mentioned that had racial overtones.

From all the talks we had, she always had good and memorable things to say about Nigel Collins. They had been happily married for 20 years and had she not been widowed by his sudden heart failure; Granny would have stayed with Nigel forever. She never married again. Now, that's a beautiful "Rose!" My brother Brandon's middle name is Nigel after his Grandfather Nigel Collins. That is one man I wish I would have had the pleasure of knowing. Maybe having his baby granddaughter in his arms before he went to heaven was his gift to me. …After all, it was 'me' he was holding, no one else—I look at that special moment as mine and his.

In my early childhood years, we lived in South Orange, New Jersey, and stayed in the family house of my real grandfather, Kenneth Williams Jr. (the first husband who Granny divorced 'lickety-split'). We kids called him "Pop Pop." Now, Pop Pop, the enterprising man that he was, had two homes built. One, down the road from his business, was just for him and his wife, Wanda, whom he married after Granny divorced him, and the second house was in front of his business and built specifically for him and Wanda's offspring—Cherlynn, Claudia, and Travis—*and* their respective boyfriends and girlfriends who also lived there. It was in this family house that my mom and I lived. Yep, it was a full house all right, but I have to tell you for the most part it was a happy house. I especially loved my Aunts, Cherlynn and Claudia. My favorite was my Aunt Cherlynn who shared a room with me and my mother. She was 10 years older than me so we were close in age in my mind. Lots of nice memories there.

As a young girl, the school I went to when I lived in South Orange, New Jersey was Stone Lake Elementary School. I loved riding the bus to school every day with my friends Tameka, Kevin, and Trevor Rhodes. The Rhodes' family lived down the street from us. Unfortunately, they grew up very poor. The Rhodes' mother had left their father when the youngest, Trevor, was about 3 years old. The Rhodes' father used to beat their mother and verbally abuse her to the point she'd had enough, and one day she just got up, packed her clothes in the middle of the night and left them all—husband and children. But the kids were very resilient at that young age, and we all took refuge in just having a great time being children; getting on the bus, we couldn't wait to see each other!

Tameka Rhodes was the oldest at 8; she was a pretty, petite, light-brown girl whose beautiful brown eyes sparkled in the sunlight. Kevin, her brother, was a tall, handsome chocolate-brown boy who was naturally built even at a young age. This was from his constant helping out in the yard—things like cutting up and carrying all the firewood to their house to fuel the stove, the only source they had to heat their home. (I'm not sure that they ever had a furnace or central heating like we had.) Trevor was the baby; he also had skin the color of chocolate like his big brother and eyes that shimmered just like his big sister.

I remember too it was fun because we hung out at my grandfather's seafood business, KW's Seafood Shack, in South Orange, New Jersey, which was on the same property as the home we lived in. These were some of my greatest childhood remembrances—playing and hanging together with my three friends. The entire time I lived there, Tamika, Kevin, Trevor, and I always rode the bus together, and rarely missed a day. That was definitely a bouquet of roses.

...But get ready for a "Thorn"—a *big one*—one I lived with for *45 years* before I was finally able to extract it. It happened when my mom Bridgette and I were moving back and forth from Indiana to New Jersey during the first, maybe, 10 years of my life. I was about 4 or 5 years old and living in New Jersey with my aunts, Cherylynn and Claudia, and Uncle Travis from my Pop Pop's side of the family when my life changed forever from the tender age of 5 on. It is the *same* story unfortunately told and heard a million times, over and over and over, BUT to each of us *pure children* it happened to, it is the single most traumatic, earth-shaking moment of our lives. It is the moment our INNOCENCE was taken from us—more accurately—*torn away* from us never to be returned or forgotten. I remember it only too well.

My mother had gone out to party at a club and left me with Granny's sister, my great aunt. It was then that my aunt's high-school-aged son (my cousin) molested me while I was asleep on her couch waiting for my mom to come and pick me up. There in my sleepy daze, I heard my older cousin come into the room and I opened my eyes to see him looming over me. Suddenly, he did something strange. He knelt down next to me on the couch where I was sleeping. I didn't know what was happening. Then all at once, I felt him ripping my onesie pajamas right off me. I froze; I think I was too scared to scream...then, the horror of it was he bent down and started licking me 'down there'...and kept doing it. I was petrified – remember, I was only a child at the age of 5. It wouldn't be till many years later that I would truly understand he had been performing oral sex in my vaginal area.

The next part is like a hazy dream. I remember my mother Bridgette had returned and was picking me up and taking me home. The next thing I recall was standing in my Granny's house unable to stop shaking as I stood beside the white deep freezer. I remember the deep freezer, because it was taller than me at the time, and I remember leaning on it for support when I was telling the adults what happened. My Granny and mother kept asking me what was wrong. I was still trembling and I remember shakily trying to point to my private parts. They pressed me further. Finally, I blurted out, "______touched me there… he-he licked me…" I put my head down, it was so humiliating and shameful!

But what was even more upsetting and stressful were these adult reactions to what had happened to me! No one stood up for me, not even my own mother. In fact, she whisked me back to Indiana just as quickly as that plane could carry me. That was Bridgette's path to dealing with any problem, RUNAWAY, back and forth, and back and forth between Indiana and New Jersey. Bridgette and Granny found my pajamas and threw them away at Granny's house in Indiana—the *onesie pajamas* my cousin tore away from me the night 'of the crime.' And it was a crime against a 5-year-old child! But… by all means, get rid of the evidence!!!!

And that's when Granny told me, "We're going to pretend this didn't happen because we don't want to cause 'a rift in the family,' so we are going to pretend it didn't happen…" and so my *should-have-been defenders* threw away the "onesie pajamas"–the only proof. Bridgette, my mother was sitting right there with my grandmother agreeing with her. –Where was the family who was supposed to protect and defend me?? – I remember them saying— "That happened in New Jersey and now we're in Indiana." And what did this little 'throwaway incident' cost me??

"For years," I could not sleep on my back. From the age of 5-years-old on, ever since it happened, I have never been able to sleep on my back. I felt as if someone would touch me once I started

sleeping; someone would hurt me if I was in this vulnerable position. I remember one time I opened up at great risk to have a conversation with my mother about it; we rarely spoke. To be honest, my mother Bridgette and I never had a relationship with each other, never communicated together but for some reason that day I felt the need to speak my heart to her because I was having these fears I was going to be molested again. I said to my mother, with great sincerity and need, "The only thing I pray, is that I'll be able to sleep on my back before I die..." I was sorry the moment the words left my mouth... My mother Bridgette threw them off like you would a fly, "Oh just get over it, Bella. *I* drank to get over it." --Good for you, I wanted to say. 'What was *I* supposed to do to get over it??'

...And I guess it was easy for my family to forget all about it because later in 1992 after we moved back to New Jersey for good in Bridgette's house, they were inviting 'him' [the cousin who did the deed] to holiday parties. I remember I questioned my mother. I was like, "What is going on...?" And she responded smugly, "Well, you run around laughing – you musta liked it." And I started to tell my grandmother but I knew my grandmother would have cussed my mother out. And Granny didn't even cuss. But when my mother said that to me—I was starting to grow up and find my own strong voice—and I responded icily, "You're a sick bitch and that's why I don't like you no matter if you're my mother or not."

Through the years, I've asked my mother twice to go to therapy with me and she told me both times, "No, because all they do is blame your mother." She said she got schooled on this because she went to therapy and all they tried to do was blame it on her mother." Well, newsflash on that one; her mother/my grandmother had nothing to do with it. Granny tried in every way to help her daughter/my mother through all the tribulations of her youth...and there were many as you are about to see. I tried to enlist my two Aunts—my Aunt Cherlynn on my grandfather's side and my Aunt Joan on my grandmother's side, but both aunts said, "Your mother's never going to change." So, at that point, I said, "You know what, I'll just do the therapy myself. She didn't want to make our relationship better, I just needed to help myself and keep moving on."

It takes a long time to 'move on.' It took me *45 loong years* and many years of therapy before I was able to reach a resolution to this sexual childhood trauma. -- You'll take the journey with me in this book, but now I was just a child at this time in my life, and I had to put my own worries and fears on the back burner because I had another traumatic experience to deal with—this time regarding my mother, Bridgette.

During this period, I was in New Jersey, around 5 or 6. As you may recall, my mom and I were living with my aunts, Claudia and Cherlynn, and Uncle Travis (and all their various mates) in Pop Pop's family home that he built for his children. Having gone through one terrifying experience at the ripe old age of 5, I just wanted to submerge myself in playing and being with my friends at school and on the bus. And I did, laughing and running and having fun as a kid. I even remember at some point—we were probably in 2nd, 3rd, and 4th grades—and we all joined a band in school and played different musical instruments. That was great fun! I wanted to play the flute, so my mother bought me one, but then, shortly after that, we moved back to Indiana; that was the end of that. I don't think I ever wanted to play an instrument again. However, it was sure fun while it lasted!

Then, one day, I came home from school—a day like any other—and I entered the family home and ran upstairs, as that is where my mom and I stayed, in an upstairs room. But suddenly, my footsteps stopped in horror as I came upon a terrible site. My mother, who was usually working for her father's and my grandfather's seafood shop at this time, was lying sprawled out on the floor, not moving. There was blood everywhere! -- And next to her was an empty Smirnoff vodka bottle turned over on its side, and next to that was a straight razor lying on the ground, and my eyes followed it to the blood all over my mother's wrists. I gasped; it took my breath away. AGAIN, I didn't know what was happening. I was trying to decipher in my little mind 'what this meant—what to do.' Quickly, I found my feet and ran as fast as I could to Pop Pop's business, the KW Seafood Shack, which was on the property behind the house.

I rushed into the establishment and ran straight to my Aunt, stammering, trying to find the right words. How does a kid come out with "Mom....Blood everywhere...Razor... Bottle... Bloody wrists, not moving'... and finally I just blurted out, "Something's wrong with my mother!!!" They all started talking at once, "What? What, Bella, what's wrong??" I'm just pointing toward the house, unable to get any words out.

I don't remember much more than this because I was so young. However, I do remember, shortly after that, being put on a plane (again!) to go to my Granny's home in Indiana. I really wasn't scared because, at that time, they would just sit you upfront in the plane, and the flight attendants would watch over the little kids. So, it was becoming the pattern, - I flew home to my grandmother's house in Indiana. They shoulda renamed the plane, "The Medi-Vac Plane," because it was always rescuing us and transporting us back and forth from some travesty.

Then I recall after a few months of Granny getting me settled and back to school in Indiana, my mom Bridgette came home. What did I know? She's there, she's on the floor all bloody; she disappears for a period, and then she's back again...as if nothing happened. This is normalcy. It wouldn't be until years later that I would come to find out that my mom had, of course, tried to kill herself, and they put her in a mental institution as they should have. After that suicidal attempt, she was finally released and moved back to Indiana *until* she decided to move back to New Jersey again. Each time we moved back to New Jersey, Bridgette got pregnant. First, it was my brother, Brandon Nigel Simmons (named after his grandfather, Reverend Nigel Collins), and then six years later, came my baby brother, Jayden Thomas.

No, that's not a mistake; both of my brothers have different last names...because they have different fathers...as did I; my last name is St. Patrick. You'll hear more about the 'three' fathers later…as well as about my mother whom I always called 'Bridgette' and rarely called 'mom,' and went months without any communication between us.

Yes, my mother, Bridgette, was a piece of work. (Just to remind you, she was one of three daughters born to Granny and her first husband, Kenneth Williams, Sr., aka Pop Pop.) I will say that my mother also saw things that would leave a lasting impression on her life as a teenager. When Bridgette rebelled in those volatile teen years, my Granny and her stepfather, Nigel Collins, sent her back to Pop Pop (her father), who was now living in New Jersey with his second wife, Wanda. It was here Bridgette would learn that her father, Kenneth Williams Sr, was an abusive man. She would hear him beating his second wife, Wanda, and my Aunt Cherlynn, who was just a baby then, would try and drown out these terrible sounds by just rocking herself to sleep.

However, at this point in my life's timeline, my mother was 'away somewhere' else, and I was put on another plane *at the age of 6* back to Indiana to Granny's house. I would have a lot of growing up to do in Indiana as *I* was growing physically, mentally, and emotionally. Having experienced a lot of "Roses and Thorns" thus far—in just the first six years of my life—let's see what else "Bella's Garden in Life" has in store as it continues to grow.

Chapter 3

Bella Blooms in Bloomington, Indiana

Following 'the traumatic childhood incident' I experienced in New Jersey, I spent the rest of my growing up years living at Granny's house in Bloomington, Indiana. Here, I would enjoy many good years being nourished and growing good bones thanks to Granny's plentiful garden filled with a variety of fresh vegetables—okra, cucumbers, tomatoes, and all kinds of greens. As a youngster, one of my favorite childhood memories growing up was tending the garden with my Granny. I enjoyed seeing how things grow. In the wintertime, we would get a lot of mice scurrying about the house—they were coming in from the fields to find warmth. My mother and grandmother were scared of the little critters and hated to throw the dead mouse traps out, yuk; however, I would do it for them because it didn't bother me, not one bit! I was a brave little thing. My brother Brandon Nigel Simmons joined our family on November 16, 1979. He carried the name of our Grandfather Nigel Collins. I was 6 at the time as there was always 6 years difference between my brothers and myself.

As mentioned, Granny was one of the greatest cooks with her sumptuous barbecues, succulent dishes, and homemade desserts. I grew into a strong, healthy girl thanks to all that wholesome food...but so did my 'expressive mouth' grow and my 'independent personality.' When I was growing up, Granny would also make and eat things that were not very appealing to me, like fried spam and egg sandwiches and potted meat. I remember she asked me to try these peculiar foods. I responded, "Granny, no disrespect, but you made it where you are so I wouldn't have to eat the poor food your momma fed you...so thanks, but no thanks." (OMG, that sounds so 'bougie.' I'm horrible, as I let out a big laugh.)

But my Granny and I had a wonderful relationship; she was a very kind, patient and understanding woman. I recall one unforgettable time that Granny let little 'Bella' know the meaning of respect and 'who the boss was' just in case I forgot and thought I was too big for my britches. Granny was in the kitchen making sandwiches for the afternoon session of Church, and I popped in and announced, "I wanna a sandwich," to which my grandmother responded, "No, you don't want a sandwich, you just ate. Go play." Granny was always right; I just *saw* and I wanted it. So, I went off and played and forgot all about it; then, a little later Granny called for me—and I think she bothered me because *now* I was into playing and didn't want to be distracted. Yea, you know, 'the nerve' of her! I was probably 6 or 7. She motioned me into the kitchen, "Okay, Bella, I packed 'em all up for the church. Here, we got extra." Suddenly my arrogant little 4-foot self, spewed back at Granny, "I ain't gonna eat a damn one of your sandwiches." My grandmother had a man friend named Thomas Stafford at this time and her eyebrows raised and she looked to her boyfriend and said, "Did Bella just say what I think she said?" Thomas answered matter-of-factly, "Yes she did."

Well, Granny spanked my little behind as she should have...and Granny was the first person who got cussed at 'by me'—and of all people—the nicest one!! That was the first time I got spanked by my Grandmother and I think I learned my lesson because I don't think she ever spanked me again. I cherish my relationship with my Granny and when she died, everything went out of control... Well, we'll get to that in due time.

It was more enjoyable when my middle brother Brandon wasn't

born yet because it was just me, my Granny and her beau, Thomas. I loved Thomas because we would go and visit him at his house, and he was like a leaky piggy bank. He would have holes in his pants pockets which resulted in an abundance of quarters being dropped all over the floor. Ha! And I would get down on my hands and knees and scramble for them and take them home with me. So, I *loved going there*. I say this with a big smile on my face!

I also really enjoyed going to church with my Granny regularly every Sunday. She always taught me about the Bible in church. Granny was in a choir and we would sing along from the church pews. –But my family let me know at a young age 'that I could not sing.' Their exact words were, "Bella, you are tone-deaf, and you can't carry a tune." They let me sing, but when I tried to join the choir, they said, "No Ma'am, you cannot sing in the choir; you can sing at home." –We are a very sarcastic type of household.

For the record at the age of 47, I actually hit a note. I remember it clearly—it was the day my brother Brandon came over and I was singing "Love Zone" by Billy Ocean. I sang the lyric, *"But when love's a guarantee, there is no mystery,"* and Brandon looked up in astonishment. I said, "Oh my God, I hit that note." And then I second-guessed myself and asked him, "Did I hit that note??" Brandon nodded in agreement, "Yeah, you did; it shocked me!" Boy, I grinned like I just sang the whole song in tune. You couldn't tell me nothin'; confidence up a thousand notches!

Another one of Granny's favorite things was she loved to bowl. My Granny and my Aunt Joan were on a bowling team, so we went bowling all the time; it was part of our lives. And Granny loved sports; she watched football, baseball, bowling and golf—but she didn't watch basketball. And whatever city we lived in that's the team she rooted for. So, when we were in Indiana, she was for the Hoosiers and when we moved to New Jersey, I think it was The Nets and the NY teams; she had a great affection for sports.

During the wintertime, we would go sledding. We would all pile up on the sled and take off zooming down the hill. Once I was on the sled with my cousin Marcus (my Aunt Joan's child); he was one year older than me. When my brothers came along, they joined Marcus and me; so, I was the only girl. At one point, it was just my cousin and me in line; he was in front of the sled and I was in the back, and we started zipping down the icy hill. For some reason, I got scared and somehow jumped off but landed right in front of the sled's path. It cut me as it continued over the top of me and ran right over the left side of my face.

Back then you had 'slides and projectors,' and I remember looking at the slide and seeing the entire side of my face was about three times its normal size. I had about 52 or 62 stitches. It messed me up bad but I healed from it. I was a kid—strong and resilient—so it was a pretty quick recovery. It did leave scars but I learned our skin sheds dead cells and makes new ones every ten years, so it was minimal damage. At the time, I probably wasn't in school because my face was triple in size. I just remember viewing the slides; it was Christmas time and I was opening my gifts and my face was still swollen like the Pillsbury dough boy. They probably let it heal and the swelling went down before I returned to school because I don't remember being teased or made fun of by the kids.

When I first got to Indiana after 'the molestation incident,' my mother was still MIA (missing in action), so I stayed with my grandmother. What would happen in the mornings is Granny would take me to my Aunt Joan's house and I would walk to school with her son, Marcus. We were always pretty close growing up. He was always a little heavy. Marcus had light skin with freckles all over his face. There was only a year's difference between us but we attended and walked to two different schools. Mine was Hamilton Elementary School. After Granny would drop me at Aunt Joan's house in the morning to go to school, she would hurry off to go to work. Then, after school, she would come and pick me up. I always used to stay with Granny; I don't recall how long my mother was away, I was so young then. Bridgette just disappeared—gone one day, time passed, and then she was back. I was too young to know or ask questions; I only knew when she did return, I was happy to see her.

The Midwest could have ferocious storms in the winter. I recall one time there was an especially bad snowstorm; it was bitter cold. My mother's sister, Aunt Joan, fell asleep and forgot to pick me up from school, which she usually did. So, I ended up walking 8 blocks to her house—all by myself in a huge snowstorm; I felt like I was walking in the North Pole! And I'm little now; I was just a little thing. To this day, I remember sitting on my aunt's vent—the heat coming up—and my teeth chattering trying to un-thaw and get warm. My Aunt Joan felt so bad; she kept apologizing, "Bella, I am so sorry." Because she had taken a snooze and forgotten about picking me up, I had to walk home by myself in an Indiana blizzard! B-r-r-r! But there would be other better days when the sun would shine and my garden would grow again.

If my Grandmother and I had the greatest relationship, my mother and I *didn't have any relationship* at all. We could not get along, ever. Honestly, I've never had a lot of respect for Bridgette. As a child, (4 going on 40), every time I looked at my mother, she was getting pregnant and then my brothers' fathers would come and leave after her pregnancy.

It's so ironic because I remember when I was an adult—about 19 or 20 years old—and we had moved back to New Jersey for good, my mother had met my stepfather, Robert Thomas. And she was all puffed-up and bragging about how my stepfather was not allowed to stay the night until they got married. I remember her saying, "I teach my kids respect by not allowing a man to spend the night if we are not married. And I'm thinking what about your sons, 'cause both their fathers were in the household when I was growing up."

To the best of my recollection—and I was pretty young at the time— this is the way it happened. My mother would live in New Jersey, get pregnant, then go back to my grandmother's house in Indiana. We would live with her at Granny's. Things would be fine for a while, then my mother would move back to New Jersey, get pregnant again, and repeat the same scenario. So, *that is why I had more respect for my grandmother than my mother because I'm looking at our mother and what she did...not cool.*

I think she did it this way because New Jersey was a safe space—where we all came from and it's safe to hang out there—but I don't know if my mom could handle raising a child on her own. And so, the comfort of living with Granny and having an in-house babysitter suited her needs just fine because the relationship between her and my brothers' fathers never worked out anyway. It's crazy. I have no recollection of my own father but I do recall what happened when my two brothers were born. Their fathers came out briefly but then skedaddled back home after their births. I can remember this because I was older.

Their fathers were men from New Jersey; they would come out to Indiana during the pregnancies. After the birth of their children, they would return home to New Jersey. They wouldn't stay long at all. I recall when my mother was carrying my middle brother, Brandon, his father moved in with us for a short time while my mother was pregnant with him. Yes, I *definitely* remember him because I accidentally opened up my mom's bedroom door while she was having sex with his father, yuk, lol! (I was 6.) The youngest brother Jayden's father stayed a bit longer. He was born 6 years later, so I was probably 12 or 13. I remember this because his father taught me how to drive. I wasn't of driving age yet but his dad was teaching me how to drive anyway. Hey, I appreciated the lessons.

Their fathers never sent child support. When my father and mother got divorced, I was about 2 when they first separated. Right after I was born, the man was having an affair on my mother. My father left and followed the woman he was cheating with to Florida. A few years later, they got divorced and he was ordered to pay $25 a week in child support (for me). He never paid, and I don't think my mom ever took the other two fathers up on it because she didn't need it. They were never in the same state as we were.

My grandmother carried the weight for *all* our fathers. – We didn't want for anything because of my grandmother. If it wasn't for her, we'd probably be living in projects because our fathers were never around and we just had a single mother. So, all the credit goes to my Granny, that I live the way I do, speak the way I do, am intelligent—all of that. That goes for all of us. Granny is the "matriarch," the one who left, made her way out, and forged a new path for the rest of us. Even as a widow when her husband Nigel died unexpectedly after 20 years of marriage, my grandmother found a respectable, stable job at the University of Indiana Department of Agriculture, where she worked consistently until 1992 when she retired. She never wavered in her responsibility to the family.

When my mother Bridgette was finished with the fathers that sired her children, she was done, period. She had several jobs. She worked in the deli at Safeway; she worked in an ink printer shop until she became employed at the University of Indiana, and then started working in the Law Library. She was able to get a job with good medical insurance, and that's how my brothers and I all got braces. Bridgette finally followed her mother's lead and stayed on working at the college.

My mother went to college after high school for a while. I don't know how long because she was having trouble in her teens and Granny sent her to live at her father's house in New Jersey. Both of my aunts, Joan and Jacqueline, went to college too. I don't think any of them finished and got a degree but my grandmother and her 3 daughters were very intelligent women. That's why we speak the way we do and articulate well because we've been raised around people who speak proper English. The adults used big words so that just trickled down. My nieces and nephews also speak correctly.

But my mother always forgot the *real story* of the "comings and goings" of my brothers' fathers. Quite frankly, her memory was shot because she was shooting heroin back then in the '70s -'80s. – My mom was not free from alcohol or drugs when she came home from the hospital and to be frank, she was on and off heroin. I know when my brother Brandon was born, I was 6 because we're about 6 years apart, and she stopped shooting heroin while she was pregnant with him. Then after his birth, she started shooting again.

With my youngest brother Jayden, my mom was too far gone,

so she shot heroin the whole time she was pregnant with him. But Bridgette told me she prayed to God and if the baby came out normal, she would stop. God must have heard her prayers because Jayden came out okay, and so she stopped when I was 12. That was the last time she got high. You have to give her credit for that one. Jayden is 40-something now, so that changed her. She did alcohol too but this time she pretty much stopped everything. When I was an adult and we all moved back to New Jersey, I never saw her drinking heavily again. At the barbecues, she might have a beer, but I never saw her drink the way she did when I was a child; she would drink 'liters' of vodka then. There were bottles strewn all over the place.

But the two boys didn't see what I saw, so they had a different relationship with our mom. They weren't privy to seeing what I saw and lived through as a young child. I guess I was the starter child where anything goes. My mother not only drank but was doing drugs when I was a little girl. I recall one time she told me—this was before Narcan—"If the heart stops, you put them in a tub; turn on the cold water and add as much ice as you have and that will jumpstart somebody's heart." I knew this life-saving fact at the ripe *old age* of 5. People really try to forget their past or try to pretend it never existed. Maybe that's why Granny and my mother told me to forget about being molested and pretend it didn't happen. The delusion of it all amazes me

Nor do I call my mother, 'Mother.' I call her Bridgette. When I was growing up I was the oldest, and I would hear people call her 'Bridgette,' so that's what I called her and she allowed me to do it. My brothers call her 'Mom.' I do call her 'Mom' in certain circumstances,- "Hey Mom, whatcha doin'?" But I also say, "Hey Bridgette," which my immediate family in Indiana knows and accepts. But when we moved to New Jersey permanently, people were looking at me and judging me, "That is so disrespectful." And I would reply, "You take it up with my mom..." She allowed it. Don't bring it up to me now – I'm grown. This is too far gone."

When I was about 35 years old, I confided to my Grandmother, "Granny, I am going to hell." And she said, "Why, Bella?" and I said, "Because I love you more than I love my parents." The wise lady responded, "You're not going to hell for that. Do you know how many grandchildren are raised by their grandparents, and they love them more? - You're not going to hell for that Bella." But I didn't know… I probably still felt guilty about that…

I am also aware my mother Bridgette had a rough beginning. My mom was the youngest of three daughters. She was born on October 27, 1952, to Granny Angela, her mother, and Kenneth Williams Jr., her father in South Orange, New Jersey. In her younger years, she went to school in New Jersey until her mother remarried Reverend Collins who was in the Air Force. Then due to her stepfather's military career, my mom had to attend several schools throughout the United States. They had to move when, where, and how often they were told.

Switching schools constantly was tough for kids in military families, no real stability, never in one place long enough to make lifelong friends, and if you did, you may have to move again. But my mom was and still is a reader (like Granny and me). She took refuge in her books; at least she had those to turn to. I remember Bridgette told me she would have to go to bed at a certain time. But when her mom and stepfather went to bed—and she was sure they were asleep—she would get up and sneak into her closet, turn on a flashlight, and read until 2 or 3 o'clock in the morning. She'd be up to the wee hours before school; she loved to read so much. And I inherited that trait because there were always books around in whatever house we were living in. My favorites were by James Patterson, Dean R. Koontz, and Tom Clancey. I was raised on those books, so we have 3 generations of women who have a great love of reading. That's a good thing we inherited.

But my mother Bridgette also had another challenge to deal with. My Grandmother was 'high yellow;' we called her '*passing*.' Before Granny died in New Jersey, we would ride along in the car, and 'All the white people' would wave at Granny because they thought my mom's mother was white and 'Bridgette, my mother' was more of a brown-skinned woman. The townsfolk—literally—did not believe that Granny was her mom, and my mom living in that biased era was picking up on all the racism. I think she was burdened with this issue a lot, being dark-skinned and her mom looking like she was—*'passing white'* as they called it—very, very fair, and light-skinned. Honestly, I think my mother had a lot of problems because of this and it affected her adversely all throughout her life.

As for my father, I didn't know too much about him or his family and to be perfectly honest, I never really missed having a father because as I've said my Granny was, "The Father of us all," and she wore the pants of the family in her own elegant way. The only time it really sucked not having a father was in school when we had "Family Tree" projects. Man, my tree was all broken up—half a tree—missing limbs like it had been through a massive tornado…which it had been. My mother never discussed any of our fathers, good or bad. There weren't any pictures of them anywhere in the house either. It was like they didn't exist. FAMILY TREE, what's that?? Ours was called, 'GRANNY'S TREE.'

The only interaction I had with my father when I was growing up was that he would call me every year on my birthday; other than that, I would not actually lay eyes on the man until I was 23 years old, but that's a story for another day.

I do know some bits and pieces about my dad. He was 6 years older than my mother and was born Michael Daniel St Patrick on September 10, 1945. His parents were William Michael St. Patrick, Sr., and Sandra Johnson, and his mother died giving birth to him. He has two brothers William St Patrick Jr and Theodore, and one sister, Lucinda. Following the mom's death, the kids were all split up and shuffled between family members due to their father having to raise the kids all alone. Given those tough facts, I guess I can understand why my father is the way he is—because he never had a mother. He has no attachment to anyone—and I think I have a part of that in me too. Those types of abandonment issues can stay with you all your life. What could I know or understand or do when my father left me? I was only two years old. I'm still trying to wrap my head around things.

I would learn my father, Michael Daniel St. Patrick, is a very handsome man, brown-skinned, 6'1," and on the thin side, weighing about 165 pounds. He was also a thug; he would pick bar fights; beat his women; he would go to jail overnight here and there; and he was definitely a ladies' man. I believe that's why my mother was drawn to him; he had that wild, unrestrained side that was very attractive to her. He was 26 and maybe more experienced than my mother who was 20 when they married.

Because we've never had a man in our household growing up, I would flip if I saw that kind of abusive behavior being done. To sit up there and see a man beatin' on my mother, we would all be going to jail. It would be a *big* problem because I wasn't raised in that kind of environment.

When my mother was a teen and sent to her father, Pop Pop's house, she saw her stepmother being beaten. My mom, a teen, offered comfort to her baby stepsister. You become used to it; it becomes your norm. You have to survive. You really can't say what you'll do until you're in their shoes. It is horrible; I see that's why all of them are messed up. I would come to learn it doesn't matter how much money you have, what you own, or what you accomplish, you can still have problems…if they're still stashed under the rug or hiding in the deepest, darkest part of you.

I am so glad I had my Granny's nurturing garden to hold on to… until I could grow my own …and that would take decades as I would find out. Bloomington is where the growing years took place. As a baby and a child, you are totally reliant on your elders to feed and house you. But I think it is only when you begin to grow and find your own feet and your own wings, that you begin to see hope and light at the end of your own tunnel.

Bloomington was like taking root of my surroundings, seeing what your foundation is—where you came from, what you're made of—how much your mother and father define your life, and pass their ghosts on to weigh you down. Before you can begin to plant your own seeds and grow your own life, you must sift through this mired mess of thorns and weeds. It was a rocky garden for me as I blossomed into a teen but I was sure of one thing—I was damn determined to grow up and move on—come hell or high water.

Chapter 4

School Daze
"A Rebel with a Cause"

When I was a child living in New Jersey, I used to play the flute in the school band. My little friends, Tameka, Kevin, and Trevor were also in the band, and we had lots of fun playing instruments and making music. But in Indiana, I didn't want to play the flute anymore. In fact, I never joined the school band again. Maybe I was growing up, or maybe I was looking for new things to do, but one thing I knew for sure —this relationship with my mother— had come to a critical breaking point. My mother used to say, "If you came out of the same hole, you are *whole,*" meaning my brothers and I were 'whole siblings' regardless of who our fathers were.

If you come from the same *hole,* you're "whole." Well, I sure didn't feel "whole"...both my mother and father were MIA. Twelve years of dysfunction and it was cumulative and overwhelming for a kid. I was done. So, when I turned 12, it was like becoming an adult for me. I was intelligent and smart and I was going to take control of my own life.

My Aunt Joan was a great role model for me. Strong and beautiful, she took control of her own life. She got a divorce from her 1st husband (my cousin Marcus's father) and relocated to St. Louis. And just as her mother my Granny did, she met a wonderful new man. Aunt Joan's new husband's name was Michael Bankole, and he would become loved and respected by my brothers and me as one of the best male role models in our lives. It was only natural that my Aunt Joan would be the one person I would go to for stability and hope. –And so, at that pivotal age of 12 years old I ran away from home.

How does a girl that young run away from the state of Indiana all the way to St. Louis, Missouri—a 4-hour drive by car—with no money or no one to help her? They would find out that I, Bella, was highly resourceful, smart as a whip, and had relentless courage—all wrapped up in a well-thought-out, strategic plan. Hell, I shoulda been hired by the CIA.

My mind was made up—I did not want to stay with my mother—not one day more! I had it all planned out. You could see that 12-year-old mind just clicking off each step methodically. Let me tell you, I had no money, *but* I had a camera—a Kodak camera—it may have been called a Polaroid and it made instant pictures back in the day. I think I got it for a birthday present, and then I also had a Walkman which was worth over a hundred dollars, so I knew I had some very expensive stuff that I could make use of.

The morning, I planned to run away, I called the school pretending to be my mother—I thought of everything—and told them that "Bella" would not be in school because 'my daughter was sick.' That worked. And then I caught the bus downtown to the Greyhound Bus Station where I hocked my camera at a nearby pawn shop. That allowed me to purchase a bus ticket from Bloomington, Indiana to St. Louis, Missouri. (Remember, I only needed a ticket for a one-way trip.)

When we reached St. Louis, I had my Aunt's address handy—I couldn't wait to get to Aunt Joan's house and see her new husband, Uncle Michael. I immediately got a cab, gave the driver the address, and rode in anticipation all the way to my Aunt's house. When we finally got there, the cab driver turned to the back where I was sitting. There was a pause. I finally spoke up and said, "Look, I don't have any money for you. I'm not gonna lie, but I have this Walkman. It's worth a hundred dollars; will you take it?" He looked at it and took it with a side glance; he probably 'made me,' a young girl, running away from home. I got out of the car, walked to the house and knocked on my aunt's door with butterflies in my stomach; the door opened and I was let in.

Then I heard my Aunt whispering wildly in the hall. She was freaking out, "What the hell's my 12-year-old niece doing here?? She's 4 hours away from home!" I called to her in the hall answering, "I ran away." My Aunt said, "Okay," in a calmer voice. "I want to come stay with you," I continued; my response was very genuine. And she was pretending everything was 'okay,' but then I heard her on the phone. She had called my mom, "Bella's here. -- I don't know, but I'll talk to her." Then my Aunt's tone changed, "She can't stay here. We don't have the room. – I'll bring her home in a few days."

My heart dropped to the floor; tears began rolling down my eyes when I heard what she said. –I should have known. It was she and Uncle Michael who had just moved down to St. Louis six months before and now her son Marcus was there with them. Yes, I was *very* disappointed…–I needed to get away from my mother and this is what I ran to. When I spoke to my Granny on the phone she told me, "Honey you could have been killed. – You're 12-years-old!" I answered Granny and my mom on the phone, "I knew what I was doing. I calculated it. I *planned* it. I called the school as my mother…." But they weren't very impressed.

When I got back home to Bloomington, Indiana, my mother was pissed, probably because she thought I was in school and here I was 4 hours away from her and she didn't know anything about it. I think my mother put me on punishment but at that point, I didn't care. I really didn't. I was 12-years-old and had run away from home for the first time. –They were my first steps out on my own, and I made it to my destination—traveling hundreds of miles all by myself. -- I'd bide my time now; I'd grow more and gain more control. – I was defiant. My mother and I can/will never get along. Period. I think I promised myself at that moment, 'I was never going to let that defeat me.'

I went back to the "School Daze," because that was my fate for the time being. There was no other alternative, so I would make the best of it. I will say that any activities my brothers and I wanted to do, my mother would push us to do them but if it was something we didn't want to do, she didn't have a problem with us quitting, so we were able to get involved in a variety of activities. My mom enrolled me in karate classes when I was about 14. But you know what? I loved it. I ended up achieving a yellow belt which was right before the orange and brown belts. And then I had a fight with my best friend; I was probably about 15, and I went to do a karate kick, and the next thing I know, she punched me two times, and then she lay out on top of me. After that, I was like, "Forget that karate." I wasn't a physical fighter.

In high school, I was an Assistant Coach for the Basketball Team. I enjoyed it, even though I didn't do it for long. Basically, I didn't go out for the team because—I'm a girly girl; I admit it—I didn't want to sweat and get my hair wet, ha! So, I did that for about one semester. Then I stopped because in my sophomore, junior, and senior days, I was enrolled in a School-to-Work-Program. I went to high school for half a day in the morning and then worked at the grocery store the other half of the day. I worked at Country Market, about a mile from the high school. I went to school from 8 AM to 12 PM, and I worked from 1 PM to 5 PM at the Market. I loved being employed and making money. As soon as I started working I told Bridgette, "You no longer have to buy me anything. I will buy my clothes and anything else I need." My first purchase was a 12-inch Emerson television for my bedroom. I was so proud of my TV.

To be perfectly honest, I'd rather be working than going to classes. School was Boring with a capital "B." It wasn't challenging for me, but I will say I had a very cool reading teacher. Her name was Mrs. Melanie Taylor. Mrs. Taylor was young, pretty, and tan. She was a Caucasian woman with a thin build and short curly brunette hair. She was one of the coolest teachers there and to top that off, she was married to an African American man. That was the talk of the school. Back then, we were progressive and integrated but there weren't a lot of bi-racial teacher relationships, at least not in my high school. Mrs. Taylor was my favorite because she was on par with me. - You couldn't put anything past her. I would sit in the back of the room—the best spot—because there I could do my own stuff and stay out of the teacher's scope. Yet even though Mrs. Taylor was my favorite teacher, I would still try to push the envelope.

I recall one day I was very bored and decided to paint my nails in class. Mrs. Taylor noticed all the way from the front that I was up to something and she slowly made her way to the back of the classroom, all the while talking about the lesson. Then suddenly she stopped when she reached my desk. Seeing what I was doing with my nails, she got a big smile on her face and said, "Bella, those are so beautiful." I replied, "Oh, thank you," a little surprised by her response. And then she took her index finger and placed it on each one of my wet nails. She ruined all the nails…and she said still smiling, "*Now*, they look even better." I told her later that I had more respect for her that day because of what she did. (Laughingly, she got me!)

My best friend was Tasha Murphy. She was pretty, smart, and tall at 5'8," physically fit with pretty, brown skin, and long brown hair. Tasha was my best friend since about 8 years old; we lived 10 houses down from each other. Either I was eating at her home with her mom and dad, Gerald and Louise, or she was at our house eating. Louise made the best barbeque ribs I ever tasted. She would marinate the ribs overnight, and then slow-cook them all day. You could smell the aroma in the air for miles. As loving as her parents looked, unfortunately they divorced when we started North Point High School, in Bloomington, Indiana, ninth grade to be exact, when we were both fifteen. Mr. Murphy had an affair and impregnated his girlfriend who was 17 years younger than him, and only 7 years older than us. Yes, she was 22 years old; Louise was devastated.

Tasha and I also hung out with Ashley and Tierra Carter; they were identical twins. They were very petite, only 5'2" tall and 100 pounds…if that…with dark skin and short thick hair, which was always done with pretty, tight curls that caressed the frames of their faces. Ashley and Tierra Carter and their family moved into our neighborhood when I was about twelve and in sixth grade. They were originally from Mississippi and they talked like it—with that twangy southern accent. They spoke so fast and 'country,' it took me a while to understand everything they were saying. I loved hanging out at their house; there were 5 of them. Michelle was the oldest sister at 15; Ashley and Tierra Carter, the twins were 12; Anthony was 10 and the only boy, and the little sister Jennifer was 7. Wow, I couldn't imagine having that many siblings.

Their parents, Reginald and Barbara Carter, opened a soul food restaurant as soon as they moved to Bloomington. They had a mom-and-pop restaurant that was very quaint and cozy. It was packed all the time—that's how you know the cooking was good. I remember before Ashley and Tierra would go to school in the morning, their parents were already preparing for the dinner meal. They would be up early in the morning cooking greens, cleaning chitlins, and seasoning up the chickens to fry. When they got home from school, Michelle worked at the restaurant with her parents a lot, so it left the twins to be parents to the younger ones, and they cooked like grown women. I was amazed they could cook so well at their ages; I could barely make a proper BLT (bacon, lettuce, and tomato) sandwich. I am definitely not a cook.

There was also my friend Joey Taylor whom I walked to Elementary school with; he was a short Caucasian boy with brunette hair and freckles. He was 'all nerd' with his plaid, button-up shirts and little glasses.

So, Tasha, the twins Ashely and Tierra, and I all shared a locker. North Point High School was beautiful; it had two floors, with an elevator, and was primarily made of glass. There were two high schools in our city: North Point High School, Bloomington, IN was on the better side of town, and there was Central High which was predominantly Black. That's the high school my cousin Marcus attended. Central High School had the best athletes by far, but the high school itself was old, ugly, and in definite need of renovation.

–I would get in trouble all the time. I was just rebellious, period. I remember I spent much of my time getting sent to the Dean's Office. Instead of suspending me—which I would have loved—they gave me 'in-school suspension' where I would still have to go to school and sit in a class all day...instead of relaxing at home and watching TV *while you're in trouble.*

My friends and I all got in trouble—the 3 or 4 of us—and we lived in the same neighborhood as the school. So, we walked to school together pretty much all those years even though I would switch back and forth from Indiana to New Jersey. We remained the same set of friends that would hang together.

One day I was in trouble for something—probably being late to class—and they sent me to the Dean's Office *again.* However, when the Dean left the room, I literally stole about a hundred school passes, *forged his name,* and placed them in the locker that I shared with my friends so if they were late to class all they had to do was 'fill in' the date and the time on the pass. Yeah, I was *bored,* but a clever, creative kid...and *generous.* I'd share the wealth with my friends.

But it wasn't long before the Dean's Department had a laser focus on that locker. When they found all the 'signed' passes inside, they called my mother. When she arrived at school, the Dean admonished her sternly, "I could actually have Bella arrested for forgery but I'm just going to put her in school suspension." My mother, to this day, says the only reason I graduated is because they wanted me *out of that school!* – I admit, *I was terrible.* This behavior of mine wasn't a 'one-on.' – The truth is I did not like school. *It is boring!* If I'm not interested in something, I get bored quickly. That's just a fact of my life. – Plus, I realized I'd rather "make money" than attend classes in school, so I really enjoyed the hell out of that High School Work Program. Being a cashier at the Country Market grocery store every afternoon made me very happy. That may have been the best part of school.

When I returned, post-runaway, it wasn't the happiest of times but one of the best memories occurred in 1986 when I was 13 and my Granny took me to my first concert. We went to see Kenny Rodgers and Dolly Parton. I'll never forget that concert as long as I live. To this day, I still love Dolly Parton. Of course, it would be Granny who would even care about taking me to my first concert—not my mother. The biggest difference between her and my mother is simple—my

Granny was "engaged." My mother's way of parenting was to help us with our homework and make sure we went to extracurricular activities. However, my mother loved to go into her bedroom and watch TV at night all by herself, while my grandmother played cards with us or sat watching movies together in the living room. Granny was actively involved with us. My mother was also a very depressed woman and she would hibernate in her room like it was a cave for her private refuge—no kids wanted or allowed.

But other things made for happy moments, wonderful flowers with many scents strewn in my path. Even though I could not live with my Aunt Joan, we had great times visiting her and her new husband Uncle Michael, in St. Louis. One of the special events we always looked forward to attending was "Tastes of St. Louis." People would have different booths featuring dishes of all kinds of foods from all over the world. You'd meander from one booth to another drawn by the amalgam of aromas. You'd have cuisine from many countries: Asia or Ethiopia, Russia or Greece, countries I had only heard about or read about in books. I would just love it. Aunt Joan and Uncle Michael would come to Bloomington, Indiana, and visit us too. We had this national event called, Hands Across America, where everyone would hold each other's hands from state to state. That was a bright spot in my teen years that I remember and appreciate.

My Uncle Michael was a wonderful man from Africa. I say it again, without reservation; he was the 'only' great male role model I've had in my life. We had no father figure so Uncle Michael became that for all of us— me, my Aunt's son, Marcus, who he took in as his own, and my brothers, Brandon and Jayden. He encouraged them all to go to school and get a college degree. He was a very positive man and he was just so kind.

To this day, I still talk to him. I remember my mother telling me a year ago, "The only person you respect is Uncle Michael." My response to her was calm and clear, "Yes since Granny died, you're absolutely right. He's the only one I respect in life because he's the only one who's shown me nothing but respect." Last year, I saw a video when Uncle Michael and his brother were visiting Africa, and his brother was asking their mother how old she was. He thought she was about 103. And the mother answered, "Only God knows." I thought, "Aw, Bless her heart." Michael and his brother came to St Louis and they both worked 2 or 3 jobs; they were very good, hard-working men. OMG, he used to make the best oxtail and I loved the way he made it. They were so delicious; I haven't had oxtail like his since then.

As for me, every day that went by, I was growing more and more rebellious. At the time, I had two Hispanic friends—Sofia and Lucia. Sofia was younger and Lucia was my age. Lucia and I went to high school together but at 16 she had become a grown woman and started hanging out on the college campus and quit school. Well, because I hung with Lucia at school and she was a prime rebel, my mother just 'assumed' I was on drugs like she was. So, I told my mom that Lucia's mother had put her in some kind of adolescent facility, but *'I'* was not on drugs. The 2nd time I came home late (from staying at my friend's house) it was a Sunday and—I didn't get a beatin,'—that's crazy. My mother didn't beat my ass. Why? That's not normal.

The next day was Monday and my mom let me go to school like everything was hunky-dory. However, when I got out of school, she was outside waiting to pick me up accompanied by my cousin Marcus—who is probably 6 feet tall and 200 lbs. If I ran, he could not catch me because Marcus always had a weight issue. Even when we were younger, my Aunt Joan would be buying his clothes in the 'husky department.' (Today, he could be a bodyguard.) My mother told me we were going to the mall. Instead, we pulled up to a treatment facility for adolescent kids.

I was admitted to Roseville Residential Inpatient Treatment for Adolescents. It was a big two-story brick building with very few windows. It almost looked like a jail. There were basically two programs there: one for mental health and the other for substance abuse. It was a thirty-day treatment center. After I was registered, the first thing they did was put me in a rubber room for the first 24 hours. I was handcuffed to a rubber mattress, which was barbaric, to say the least. I guess that was a precaution in case I was on drugs or wanted to hurt myself. I was supposed to be there for 30 days.

But after that it was easy. I was eventually put in a room with my roommate Kelly Littlejohn. She was a 17-year-old Caucasian girl, very thin, blue-eyed, blond-haired, with freckles on her very sunken face; it looked horrible. You could tell she was beautiful before the drugs. She told me her drug of choice was PCP (Phencyclidine) or as it's known on the streets—"Angel Dust"—which she'd been on since the age of 14. Kelly told me she had ended up with the wrong crowd when her parents divorced and one thing led to another and she became hooked. I felt for her, Kelly seemed like such a good kid; it's so sad to be strung out at such a young age.

Our daily routine at the Adolescent Recovery Center consisted of a shower, breakfast, and group therapy where we all had to participate; then we had a break for about an hour before lunch. I would have to say the food there was great! All the cooks were predominantly African American and they were in the kitchen cooking up a storm. Each meal was buffet-style, and there were so many options. We had rotisserie chicken, bacon cheeseburgers, or personal pizzas, and steamed salmon with vegetables. After lunch, we would have another hour break, and then it was back to group therapy for the afternoon. Missing school and getting a break from Bridgette, I was not mad at all until 7 days later.

The first 7 days they test you for every drug known to man. All my tests came back 'negative,' so they cut me loose and told my mother, "We can't keep her. She's not on drugs. It's just adolescence." The real reason I was acting out is quite simple—I did NOT want to be around my mother. Ever since I came out of the womb, we just never got along. As adults, when my grandmother was around, she made us be 'cordial' to each other, but when my Granny died, it was a wrap; we'd go our separate ways.

At the facility, I was called to my counselor's office, Mr. David Bradford. Mr. Bradford was a middle-aged Caucasian man with short brown hair, cut into a bob style. I was a little confused; he reminded me of Moe from the "Three Stooges." Mr. Bradford had a deep, baritone voice, but it was still friendly. He gave me the news, I had passed my drug tests showing I was not on any drugs, so they were going to have to kick me out of the program. I was certainly disappointed; they assessed me with just 'normal adolescent behavior,' and I was released that same day.

When I was in the adolescent facility, the kids would have groups that we all had to attend. This was interesting because there were kids from all kinds of families and they all had different stories to tell. After I got out of the facility, the main thing I told my mother was, "That was the best cookin' I ever had!" It turns out that one of the girls I went to high school with—well, her mother worked at the facility and she would give me double servings of food! Being in the adolescent facility for a week, I not only got a whole week's break from school but 'I ate better than I've ever eaten.' Laughingly, I say, "That's what you call turning a negative into a positive!" No, I didn't hold it against my mother for putting me in there. I'm not on drugs. The truth is: "I just don't like you," ...but I couldn't tell her that to her face. But that's exactly how I thought and felt.

Despite this state of our relationship or lack of one, there were still times when a young woman needed a mother. *I still reached out,* like the time my period came, and I didn't know how to put the tampon in correctly. When I was thirteen I woke up to find blood in my bed, I knew my period (menstrual) had come. I immediately went into my mother's bedroom, waking her up. At that point, Bridgette was working the overnight shift, 11 PM to 7 AM at an ink printing company. I woke her up and told her my period had come. She rose on her elbow, half asleep, and told me to go put a tampon in. I went into the bathroom and grabbed the tampon. I tried to comprehend the instructions on the box: I opened up the tampon, spread my legs apart, and shoved it into my vagina. It was painful as hell! I walked back into Bridgette's bedroom, bowlegged like a cowboy, and shook her until she completely woke up. I said, "This hurts. I can't wear this." She definitely was pissed off now. What was she getting mad at me for?? I didn't make my period come on that day. And to top it off, she tried to make me feel stupid because I didn't know that you shouldn't insert the "plastic part of the tampon" into your vaginal area.

She finally got up and went to the Rite Aid store and bought me some Stayfree maxi pads. I was so thankful. Years later, I found out I was not even supposed to use a tampon due to the fact I had never had sex. They are not recommended until you are sexually active.

And she sure as hell didn't tell my brothers and me how the 'birds and the bees worked.' The topic of sex—which she surely knew something about—was not a topic she cared to discuss with her growing children. She never told us anything about taking precautions so you wouldn't get pregnant or with my brothers 'how not to get a girl pregnant.' Later in life when I was an adult and broached her with the topic of sex education in teens—the proverbial "talk" you have with your children—she just flipped it off again. "You learn by yourselves, from other people just like I did." Not cool. And I guess Granny just deferred this important topic to the 'mother.' I stopped liking my mother years before even that, but the final provocation of hers came when I was 16 years old—the "motherload" that broke the camel's back and turned my intense dislike of her into hate.

It had to do with my father. The one and only thing my father would do is call me every year on my birthday. (Remember, I never physically laid eyes on the man…until I was 23.) There were no pictures in the house of my father, or my brothers' fathers for that matter. My mother never talked ill about our fathers but she never discussed them so I guess I…don't know what I thought. But I clearly remember when my dad called me on my 16th birthday, I was so happy and equally angry.

I asked my father if I could move in with him. Now, that was either desperation or pure survival because anything would be better than living with my mother—even living with a stranger, who my father was. The one thing I did know about my father was that he had moved to Tallahassee, Florida, remarried, and had a stepdaughter living with him. The daughter belonged to his current wife and was my age; that was appealing as I didn't have any sisters. I told my father point blank, "I don't want to stay with my mom anymore. I don't want to be here anymore. Can I move in with you? Can I fly out there?" His response was instant, "Yeah, of course." I don't know if I was surprised but I knew I got the answer I wanted. Without a second's hesitation, I gave my mom the phone, went into my room, and started packing up all my clothes.

After she hung up, my mother walked into my room, saw me putting my clothes into a suitcase, and asked, "What are you doing? Matter-of-factly I answered, "My father said I could come stay with him. I'm flying out there." "No," she answered. He said, "He can't pick you up." What?? What are you talking about? -This time *I was totally pissed!!!* "Why would this man lie to me?" I confronted her right to her face. She walked out of the room without an answer.

It would only be 'years later' that I would come to find out my father *worked at the airport*—until the day he retired. My father would tell me when I was an adult and asked for an explanation, "I told her to send you. How could I not pick you up when I work at the airport??" I repeated this conversation to my grandmother and said, "Granny—my Dad told me—he said I could go live with him, and my mother said—" Granny stopped me in her insightful way, "Bella girl, you know that Bridgette was not going to send her 1st born..." But that's messed up because now Bridgette had me hating my father, and I'm thinking he lied to me when it was really her… -"Two thorns" but I always try to remember 'the Roses.'

Chapter 5

To Catch a Thief & Mad Dog "...Love is in the Air"

When I walk down Memory Lane, I always remember this special boy from my grade school years. His name was Joey Taylor and from Kindergarten through 5th grade I would walk to this boy's house and then we would walk to school together. This was in Indiana, so I recollect the snowy winters and how we would laugh and talk as we walked through the snow drifts to and from school. Then I'd drop him off at his house. He must have transferred or moved somewhere else because, during the middle school years, that's when I started having female friends. But I will always remember him... Joey Taylor. Recently, I tried to look him up on Facebook but I couldn't find him. I always wondered what had happened to him. He's probably the CEO of some internet company; he was always a nerdy, little guy. Smart as a whip, he's no doubt super-rich, ha! Yeah, it was so cool because we were best friends. There are just people who remain special in your life. They're only there for a short time but you always remember them no matter how much time passes.

And then there are times in your life and people you remember for 'other reasons.' It must have been around 1988 when I was around 15 years old that I started hanging out with girls from the 'less desirable side of town.' Boy, that turned out to be a mistake, and the irony is I met them at vacation bible school which I attended every summer for one week at the First Baptist Church of Unionville.

One night, they introduced me to my first party on the college campus. And I got my initiation into drinking Mad Dog 20/20 grape-flavored wine—the drink of choice for the college crowd because it was cheap and it would get you wasted quick. Oh, brother. I drank it down and it was damn disgusting at first, but as the night wore on, it grew on you and it started tasting better, and better. By the time I got to the party, I was well on my way to getting wasted. I remember dancing and dancing and then going outside to throw up, yuk... and then memories get pretty fuzzy. The last thing I can recall was waking up in the back seat of my mother's car and Bridgette helping me out of the car into the house and into bed. When I awoke the next morning—totally oblivious to what had happened—my mother told me I had passed out and she got a call from one of my friends to come pick me up. I respected the fact that my friends called her, but it scared the hell out of me not knowing what could have happened while I was blacked out. You'd think I woulda learned my lesson... considering the company I was keeping, but no...

These girls were what I called 'semi-professional thieves.' We started hanging out at the mall on the weekends. One time, we went to Kohl's Department Store. And in these girl cliques, you had to prove your worth. You want to 'hang with the cool girls,' then you gotta show your stuff. This was *my* day—I was going to demonstrate my skills on the art of thievery. But of course, I Bella, was a *virgin thief* and have never stolen anything in my life—I never needed to—anything I ever asked for or wanted within reason, I was given. However, today, I had to choose something to steal...what am I going to choose... I decided to steal a necklace. - I wanted to impress the pros.

I observed with a keen eye how this was done. One by one the 5-girl-member theft ring surreptitiously put things in their pockets, and shoes. I even watched as one girl put a piece of jewelry in the palm of her hand and skillfully put her gloves on, so smoothly it wasn't detectable. Then she proceeded to walk right out of the store, a perfect performance, with no alarms going off or security alerted. Now the girls were looking at me and I knew the baton had been passed to me - the jig is up. - Now it's my turn to show what I'm made of!

My heart was beating a mile a minute, but I can't back down now—how *uncool*, not to mention 'humiliating,' that would be. So, I quickly grabbed a fifteen-dollar silver chain and dropped it in my purse and I walked towards the door just as nonchalantly as I could. I thought I would be home-free as soon as I got through the first set of doors. WRONG! Beep! Beep! Beep! The alarm started going off immediately, and before I could even turn around to see if I had a chance to run, they had my sorry butt—a security guard was right behind me grabbing my arm. I can still hear his voice in my head, "Ma'am you need to come with me." (I had graduated from *a young lady* to a *ma'am* in less than a minute.)

All I could think of was *fuck*! Bridgette is going to kill me. The guard led me into a room with a desk, a phone, and a few security cameras. I was told to wait; a female security guard would be coming soon. Once she entered, I could see I wasn't getting a shred of sympathy from this woman; this was no joke. And a few minutes later, she had me empty my purse on the table and there was the shiny culprit—a fifteen-dollar necklace—staring up at us, just as plain as day. Now the real fucked-up part is I had twenty-six dollars in my wallet!

Needless to say, Bridgette, was pissed when she picked me up. Interestingly, I didn't get a beating this time. I think by then she was over putting her hands on me and the truth was, my mother was just damn embarrassed and confused at why I did what I did. To be perfectly honest, I was just trying to fit in. I had never been in trouble, so when I went to court for my misdemeanor theft charges, I was given probation for a year before judgment, which meant I had to report to my probation officer once a month. The other stipulation was I could not get into any new trouble, which I complied with and there were no further problems.

Since we all lived in the same house, my Granny knew that I got caught stealing, and yes—my grandmother was rightly pissed, as she should be. Here I am actin' the fool—I was mortified, even ashamed, because I had the damn money, and I could have easily paid for it, with money to spare! – I was just tryin' to be cool, hangin' with the wrong crowd. But I started looking at my choices. When I was with these girls, I got caught stealing or I got drunk on campus, which I really did not like. 'Blacking out,' I was not in control; I couldn't even remember where I was or what I did! After that, I was like, *'I'm'* done with them. I'm not a drinker--that's what they do. I'm not a thief--that's what they do. That's all it took for me— "First time, shame on you; second time, shame on me." I was just 15, and I wanted to hang out with them, being cool. -Why spend your money, when you can steal it? Rebellious stuff but my choices had consequences.

My mom had already sent me to the adolescent facility, and every time I did something—runnin' away, stealin', actin' a fool—everybody was involved! My grandmother—well, Granny was at home with my brother the night I got inebriated out of my mind. The whole family's not going to come out at 1 o'clock in the morning; that's why my mother came by herself to pick me up from that college drinkin' bash. I'm only 15 years old. I admit it; I had no business being at a college party in the first place, drinkin' like a fish. I was wrong, 100 percent wrong. But I learned anytime we got in trouble, it was a "family thing." Basically, my grandmother stepped in as the father figure. We would sit down and have a family talk, all of us—as in Granny and Bridgette, the two parental figures. We would talk about household conduct and *misconduct.* I come away not only *actin' like a fool but lookin' like a fool. And I didn't like it...*

So, it was back to School Daze again. But I didn't really *try* in school—just as long as I passed, I was okay with that. I really didn't care. And the beat goes on... I continued to have a toxic relationship with my mother. I ran away again. This time I went to school on a Friday and after school and work I went to my friend's house and stayed for the weekend. I eventually meandered home on Sunday afternoon when I was good and ready. I'd usually get a beatin' when I appeared late and didn't honor my curfew, except for the one time I came home late on a Sunday and Bridgette *didn't* give me a beating. The next day she surprised me and took me to the adolescent rehabilitation facility.

There is another major reflection regarding my mother I still wince at—when my mother beat me like a man, for no reason. That's when my feelings for her *really* turned to hate. I was fifteen and my mother beat me like I was a bitch on the street, all because I was in the mirror concentrating on something. She entered the bathroom directing me like a drill sergeant, "I need you to clean that bathroom today." ...Well, I wasn't having it that day, and I said, "It's not my bathroom; you can clean it." I didn't think Bridgette was going to whale on me with such brutal force. The next thing I knew she punched me on the side of my face near my temple with such force that I landed in the bathtub, and she didn't stop there but continued to repeatedly punch me. All I could do was put my hands up to protect my face like a boxer, trying to block every punch she threw. I remember it took three people—my Granny, cousin Marcus, and brother Brandon to pull her off me. That really did it... My dislike turned to hate for my mother that day as never before.

Now, you could say that what I said to my mother was disrespectful but I think even Granny checked her on that fit of rage. It was uncalled-for behavior. Bridgette didn't need to beat me like I was a grown man for that—I was *soo* 'over that woman.' That's why I kept trying to run away. Don't get me wrong. My mother made sure we were fed, that we didn't want for anything within reason; anything we needed, we got...but my mother did not know how to love us. I don't even think she had self-love for herself. So, I'm just blessed to have a grandmother who raised me under *her roof.*

And I found out something else. Through therapy in later years, I learned the independence I have deep within myself—manifested itself that day—because *they, my parental surrogates,* did not protect me. That was the day that I became fiercely 'independent.' I know this because I was diagnosed as being "too independent." I refuse to ask anyone for help because I don't want to be disappointed, so I do everything myself. If I can't do it, it doesn't get done. *I don't ask.* Period.

Did my mother ever apologize for her behavior (beating me down like I was a 'man')? Well, I don't ever remember my mom apologizing to me directly. However, when I was in rehab—sometime later—the therapist talked me into giving her permission to talk to my mom. She would call and speak to Bridgette after our conferences. One day, the therapist called my mom just as I was walking out of the room because I had stipulated, "I don't want to be in the room while you are talking to my mom." And I heard my mother say, "I've made a lot of mistakes with my daughter." Now, she never told *me* that but admitted it to someone else, and that's the only time I ever heard my mother say anything to that effect. Maybe that's saying I'm sorry in some way, and my mother also told the therapist she dealt with my molestation incident by drinking. "Well, that ain't helping *me,* Ma'am." My mother told me that when I was an adult and my response was, "Well, you were drinking long before that, so let's not go there, Bridgette."

My mother is a thorn in my heart. No, more accurately put, she's a "bee stinger in my heart." Do you know that a stinger contains a muscle that continues to burrow into your body once you've been stung? That's why a bee sting prolongs the pain. That is a more definitive description of how my heart feels regarding the mother who gave me birth.

When I was a little whisp of a girl, Bridgette would be drinking 'liters' of vodka. She would drink every night when we lived in New Jersey. My mother was truly an alcoholic and heroin addict back then, and she was heavy on both. Later on, she would tell me my rebellious behavior reminded her of herself back when she was on drugs. The big difference was *I wasn't on drugs.*

I try to be understanding, I really do. I try to give my mother credit when credit is due. I think my mom had some very deep issues before I came along, and I also take into consideration that Bridgette was only twenty years old when she had me. As far as I'm concerned, she was a child too. My father was a grown man at twenty-seven. I don't know when they actually married or even how long they were together before I came along. The only thing I do know is that they were married when I was born. Twenty and twenty-seven years old—maybe that's a big age difference back then—but I didn't have anything to do with it; that was between them. On the other hand, when it all began my mother was grown, and you can't tell a grown person what to do.

Bridgette's father definitely had his own issues too. He hit my grandmother one time and that's all it took. Granny was long gone. Pop Pop used to beat the second grandmother constantly. That's the time that Bridgette had to go stay with her father, Kenneth Williams, in New Jersey and witnessed my Aunt Cherlynn who was the youngest of her dad's second family—rocking herself to sleep because she would hear her father beating her mother. In New Jersey, they beat their partners- that was just normal behavior back then. Bridgette was a rebel too so my Granny sent her to live with her father who in turn was beating his wife in front of his own children. What a generational, dysfunctional mess...

I'm not sure if my mother was taking pills for depression or not. I do remember Granny telling her one time, "Bridgette, you ain't foolin' anybody. You went from heroin to alcohol, to pills." So, my mom ended up getting hooked on prescription pills from our doctor. That's one thing I can say about my grandmother—she never pulled any punches. She told it how it was.

My Aunt Jacqueline, Granny's oldest daughter, as I've mentioned was a flight attendant. She flew all over the world and had the best of everything. However, when Aunt Jacqueline got 'above herself'—and did something to demonstrate she was 'higher' than the rest—well, Granny let her have it. – "You're only a glorified waitress in the air!" and my grandmother would walk off, her words trailing behind her..."So bring it down a notch."

Granny called her 'a glorified waitress in the air!' Ha! Granny knew how to read somebody. 'Don't get above yourself, 'cuz she will bring you back down to earth in a hurry.' *"It's cool to be confident...but don't get arrogant."* Granny always made sure we knew The Lord and taught us to be respectful. "Treat others with respect—the way you want to be treated." She didn't play at 'getting above yourself.' She would let you know, "Don't forget where you came from."

But on some things, Granny deferred to 'my mother' to do the teaching, like having discussions with me or my brothers about contraception or prevention of pregnancy, which she never did. This isn't important information for teenagers?? With my mother's and Granny's generations, it was as if 'sex' was a taboo topic--just *"figure it out yourself."* God forbid you mention "s-e-x" out loud.

Today, it's just the opposite; it's *too* out there! Back then, there were magazines that were kept behind the counter and that was the basis of your sex education. Now sex is prevalent everywhere. It's sad because kids today don't understand the meaning...that 'the act' means something—something very intimate and special—not just "Wham, bam, thank you Ma'am." It goes to the very core of our society—no morals, no manners, no respect. There used to be a phrase, "Respect your Elders," and people would say, "I'm sorry," and they knew the meaning of being courteous. That is *past tense*, no more. No one has respect for anybody. It doesn't matter if you're 100 years old, or you're 20; they have 'no' respect for anyone or anything. Teachers can't say anything to their students or they get attacked. It's a perilous journey today.

But when I look back at my life as a teenager, it wasn't so easy either. A lot was going on too: lies and deception, school and boredom, rebelliousness and trying to fit in, thievin' and drinkin', and trying to run away 'cause you just can't bear one more minute living where you are. BUT somehow God always throws a "Rose" into my garden that is strewn with rocks, weeds, and thorns aplenty.

A beautiful, unforgettable event happened when my family and I went to New Jersey the summer before I graduated high school. We had all driven down from Indiana to New Jersey for the 4th of July weekend—me, my grandmother, my mother, and both my brothers. It was an eleven-hour drive one way, very long but so much fun. The whole ride there I remember my mom Bridgette listening to Billy Ocean's new tape. My favorites were "Love Zone," and Freddy

Jackson's "You Are My Lady." We listened to our songs in between listening to whatever radio station we could find on the radio.

My fragrant, sweet-smelling "Rose" was—*I fell in love*—and had a beautiful summer romance with my very first boyfriend, Kevin Rhodes, who eventually I would marry. You remember that handsome little Kevin? He was the one I rode the bus to school with every day along with his brother and sister, Trevor and Tameka. That summer Kevin was working for my grandfather at his well-known establishment, KW's Seafood Shack, in South Orange, New Jersey. At the time, there were a lot of young kids and adults working for my Pop Pop.

To be honest, I think Keven and I were drawn together because of *familiarity*. We would catch the bus together every day when I was younger and lived there. His family all lived right up the street and we all went to the same school together. It was like family. Kevin worked at my grandfather's business as a boy and we all grew up together. In fact, Kevin actually lived in the same house that my father grew up in. It was a close-knit family of sorts.

Kevin and I went together for the entire summer. I was only supposed to be there for a week but after what transpired I didn't want to go back to Indiana, so I talked my mom into letting me stay with Aunt Cherlynn in New Jersey for the rest of the summer. My Aunt and I were only 10 years apart so I always felt closer to her.

I really looked up to my aunt. She was so laid back and cool. Cherlynn was gorgeous; she was 5 '6" and 150 pounds with flawless, caramel-complexion skin, beautiful dimples, and short auburn hair. Built like a brick house, when she walked, her hips switched with a purpose, and all the men were after her. I remember I would follow her around whenever she was home. I wanted to be Aunt Cherlynn when I grew up.

So, my family headed back home to Indiana without me, and my first boyfriend and I experienced the beauty and romance of First Love for the whole summer. We were inseparable. We dated; we would hang out; we went to movies; we ate together and did all the stuff young people do when they're in love. I was at his family's house; he was at mine. It was a lovely summer romance in 1989 when I was 15. Kevin would come over to Aunt Cherlynn's every day after working for Pop Pop; we would hang out, go to the fair, bowl, go to the movies, anything I wanted he made sure I had it. It was so much fun. He was my first boyfriend, and I fell in love, and so did he!

We found places to be together just by ourselves, and then well, the end of summer came and I had to fly home...but I wasn't really sad because this time I would be carrying with me some very sweet, fine memories of First Love...

Chapter 6

Back to Mayberry The Good, the Bad and…

I returned to Indiana following that Summer of Love and completed my last year of high school. It was pretty uneventful. However, I graduated in 1991 and received a diploma from North Point High School in Bloomington, Indiana. It was a milestone of sorts, and my whole family attended my graduation ceremonies just as they would if I was in a play or any school event, or my brother was playing in a basketball game. That was a 'given;' my family supported everyone's affairs. There were no reasons or excuses for not being there.

Considering how I felt about school all those years, it's probably not surprising that I had no interest in going to college after graduation. Surprising or not, my family was supportive of my decision. What I did want to become—more than anything else—was very simple. I wanted to be a 'wife and a mother'—a stay-at-home mother. That is what I wanted to be. And I think that vision stayed in my mind for a long time.

In 1992, following my graduation, my mother moved us back to New Jersey for good. It was like moving back to *Mayberry*; no one locked their doors and everyone knows your name, just like in *Cheers*. Though in a few ways, I was like a duck out of water. Firstly, no matter where I go, I usually stand out. I just do. At 5' 3" and 130 pounds, I am petite in stature compared to the rest of my family. My brothers are 5'10" and 5'11"; my mom is 5'5". Everyone is of normal height. I take after my father's people. My uncles on my dad's side are about 5'5"; they're about 85 years old, and they look 50—little petite men, very tiny. You can tell a St. Patrick by the nose and the short height. Our family is easy to identify because we all look alike. I am blessed to have the best of both worlds. I get my intelligence from my mother's side and my good genes from my father's side of the family.

Secondly, I speak differently than most people in *Mayberry*. When I moved back to New Jersey, some of my family members would often look at me with a puzzled look and say, "...What did you just say?" It's ironic because I would look at them curiously when they'd say, "You sound like a white girl." "Uh, no. It's just called proper English. Anyone can speak that way; you just have to be taught."

It's not a 'race' thing at all, thank you very much! Yes, I had to set them straight real quick; I was raised in a middle-class Indiana community, so we had a mixture of all heritages—Black, White, Asian, everything. Our schools were integrated; I had Black teachers in my high school. Proper English was taught and spoken in my home, and correct pronunciation and grammar were used. It's a form of homeschooling and a lifestyle choice that affects the whole family.

Honestly, it was because my Granny had the foresight and courage to move away from *Mayberry* early in her life, becoming educated so that we could have a middle-class upbringing and become accustomed to a different social status. That is why we are well-spoken and have class—some of us more than others, some of us not at all—but Granny always said, "Money can't buy you class." There are times I feel like I exuberate class, and then there are times that I act like I have no home training whatsoever.

My grandmother picked herself up and got away from her humble beginnings and was able to give us a life—and a lifestyle—that she never had. I appreciate her every day of my life; if it wasn't for her, we would not be where we are. Granny used big words, and her vocabulary just trickled down through the family. My nieces and nephews speak in the same way. I've always been around people who speak English properly, and the people who never left *Mayberry* look at you differently.

I give my grandmother the utmost respect and credit she deserves because she came up during the Depression Era. She was raised in a 2-bedroom house that was home to 12 children— twelve children in two bedrooms—so she elevated herself. Can you imagine having a dozen siblings in total? One of her sisters, Aunt Estelle, died in a house fire. Granny and her sister Aretha were the only ones that made it out—all the way—from the small-town environs and mentality; it was a tiny country town in the Northeast.

When I researched it recently, it has a general population of 3,500. Back then, to survive, some of the siblings were either cleaning houses or driving for white people. Even though my Granny and Aunt Aretha moved away from New Jersey to further their education and really do something with their lives, the siblings who stayed were hearty intelligent souls and still flourished without higher learning. They all became successful homeowners. They should be commended too.

One of Granny's sisters, Aunt Dorothy, just recently passed away at 91. For many years, Aunt Dorothy was scared to death to get on an elevator, let alone take flight in an airplane. So, my Granny visited her sister's daughter a few times while she was in the Navy and stationed in California. Eventually, Aunt Dorothy overcame her fear, and the next thing we knew, Aunt Dorothy and Granny were flying back and forth to California all the time! Dear Granny had that special touch where she could gently coax people out of their fearful places. Maybe that was one of her greatest attributes; Granny didn't push you but guided you until you could find the confidence to let go and find your own way.

Granny's visionary way of looking at the world—wanting to explore places near and far—filtered down to one of her daughters, my Aunt Jacqueline. As you've learned, Jacqueline became a flight attendant and saw the world, and Granny was right behind her. Besides traveling statewide with her husband, Nigel, when he was in the military, Granny continued her love of travel even after she became a widow. When her nieces and nephews—her sisters' kids were in the military—she would hop on a plane and visit them wherever they were stationed. One was in Guam; one was in Japan. Granny's sisters were afraid to fly and see their kids, but my grandmother would fly to the most exotic places to visit her nieces and nephews. Granny probably would have volunteered for space travel had that option been open to her!

I must admit, when my mother Bridgette moved us back to New Jersey in 1992, I was loving life and enjoyed having all my family around, unlike growing up in Indiana, where it was just the 'immediate family.' My brothers would attend high school in South Orange, and that was a big family affair, and we would attend all their games. Granny moved back to New Jersey too. Her husband Nigel died in 1973, and Granny stayed in Indiana until 1992, when she retired from the University of Indiana Agriculture Department as an executive assistant to the Dean. Then she relocated back to New Jersey.

When my mom relocated us back to New Jersey, I also decided to rekindle my relationship with Kevin (my first summer love). However, you would be incredibly surprised at how much difference one or two years make since I'd seen him last. There was a huge problem! Kevin was no longer the sweet, respectful young man who had worked for my grandfather; he had become a mid-level drug dealer. Kevin wasn't shit because he was no longer a good man, but to the streets, he was "the shit." Kevin had the most beautiful smile, but he went and got some damn "gold teeth" to solidify the image. I was so mad! What?? What did you do? Most of his family have gold teeth....so I should have expected it.

Here was the Kevin I went to school with when we were very small children, so I knew his mother had abandoned him. I knew him when I was back and forth from New Jersey to Indiana—from the age of 5 and 6 on. It's a miniscule town. Now, there are only 3,500 people in that town, so back in the day it was probably 500 people that made up the population. It really was like *Cheers;* everybody knows your name as well as *'everybody's business,'* because your neighbor lives three doors down and she's always looking out the window, watching who's coming in and out of your house. Nosy, that type. We were all kind of raised like we were family. Kevin lived right up the street from my grandfather's house.

The young man I'd left behind in the Summer of Love, the wholesome teen who worked in Pop Pop's actual yard where they steamed crabs by the bushels along with shrimp and oysters depending on the season, had turned into Dr. Jekyll and Mr. Hyde! What the fuck is going on?? Now, he was dating a forty-year-old woman. This was insanity to me. He was only twenty years old but now was weighed down with a pocket full of money—age didn't matter; they could care less. It was only about the money.

I was still young (and nobody could tell me anything), and I was being ruled by my heart and emotions, not my head. (What did I know? I've only been in love once...) and I decided, "I guess we will all go together because 'I was still in love with him and I was not giving up that easy.'" Within two months of my moving back home to New Jersey, the 'older' woman decided to back down. (She was smarter and older than me, and surprisingly mature.) She eventually told Kevin in a very rational manner, "I know you love her, so you might as well be together." And that was that, and Kevin and I did just that.

In January 1993, I did something unexpected. I was seeking a lifetime career opportunity, so I joined the United States Navy as a Seamen Recruit. I finished my boot camp training in Chicago, Illinois, and was transferred to the base in Pensacola, Florida. My grandfather, Kenneth Williams Jr., was in the military, and I think he had gone to the same boot camp. He had a friend; I think his name was John Gibbs. He was the 1st Black Admiral in the Navy, so when I was in Boot Camp and I was stressing out and was calling home to speak to my family, they told my grandfather. My Grandfather Williams, aka Pop Pop, made some calls, and Admiral Gibbs himself came to Chicago to my boot camp. Admiral Gibbs sat down personally with me, and we had a long talk. Afterward, I remember my Boot Camp trainer saying, "You must be a real fuckin' big deal' because I've been here ten years and 'no one' is allowed—NO ONE—is allowed visitors on this training base." That's exactly what he said, "You must be a real big 'Fuckin' Deal." Here's a white countryman in the South, flabbergasted, and he was so 'country' the way he expressed it.

Then one night I called back home to New Jersey and couldn't reach Kevin, and I panicked; I knew this fool was up to no good. I called my mom right away and became quite emotional. I was crying, loudly expressing, "I don't want to be here anymore; I will kill myself if I don't get out of here."

My roommate heard me crying and came over and hugged me. She gave me a pep talk, telling me how she too was homesick when she first got here. That calmed me down—it really did—so much so that my roomie and I started watching a movie and were really enjoying it until we began to hear numerous firetrucks and police sirens heading our way. We walked quickly to the window as the 1st responder sirens grew closer and louder until we heard the commotion downstairs right below us. The police and ambulance were there for me!

My mother Bridgette had called down to the base and told them I had threatened to kill myself. OMG, I was immediately taken to a mental institution on base. Here, for the first time in my life, I experienced actual bonified crazy people—most of them had lost their minds during the war. I was there for seven days and then was released from the Navy with an Honorable Discharge stating that 'I was too immature to be there, but I could come back if I wanted to when I had gained maturity.' In my mind, I knew I would never return. Yet, when I looked back, that was probably one of the dumbest mistakes I've ever made—leaving a stable military career. It's only when you get older you realize, "I could have traveled all over the world. I was just too immature at that time—I could have had a great career and seen the world like my Granny did."

And to be honest, all I really wanted was a secretarial-type administration position, but my recruiter didn't really inform me properly and screwed me over, as they probably do a lot of naïve recruits. He told me I should go in as a Seaman's recruit, and that way I could experience all different kinds of jobs and wouldn't be stuck doing the same job for my entire four years. Come to find out that meant you got the shitty jobs, so I was either painting on a ship for a month and then get switched over to the cooking duties, so, "no," you should always have an actual career in mind when you go in if you can.

But back then, they'd say whatever they needed to get you in the door and sign on the dotted line. It's not a 'woman thing' either; it was 1993, so women were accepted. I was signed up for 4 years; I did it in 4 months. I passed my boot camp, and I was transferred to Pensacola, Florida, and that's when I acted up like a fool, cried, and got taken away to the loony house. End of story...well, at least for 'my military career story;' there's plenty to come. I was just entering the gates of the forest, as Dorothy did in *Oz*. "What the hell is next?" "Oh, a lot, my dear. A whole lot!!"

Well, believe it or not—I did find a 'Rose' waiting for me—when I returned home to New Jersey after my big 4-month stint in the military. Kevin and I moved in together, and I got to say, "That was great!" I had enrolled in the local community college and was taking classes in basic computer training. At the same time, I was working at the Levi's clothing store. My life was full, and I was enjoying the hell out of it, and *also* I never paid a bill (thanks to Kevin's special mode of employment)! I could get used to this lifestyle.

Like the genie in the bottle, anything I wanted would appear—clothing, jewelry, things for the house, you name it. In the beginning, when Kevin wasn't being that arrogant 'drug dealer,' I would come home—we had a nice apartment then—and Kevin had been out shopping and would have 5 or 6 outfits waiting just for me.

However, that 'beautiful rose' was soon to shrivel. One day I recall Kevin picking me up from work, and we gave my 16-year-old co-worker Keisha a ride home. A few months later, I would find out this fool-man was fucking my co-worker the whole time we were working together. My favorite aunt on my grandfather's side, yes, Aunt Cherlynn, was the one who enlightened me. (As mentioned, she was 10 years older than me and heavy in the streets at the time.) I remember I was off work that day when my aunt broke the news to me. The steam reached a boiling point within seconds. I went directly to Levi's job site…beat Keisha's ass, broke my nails, scratching her face with a vengeance, and was put out of the store and fired immediately.

On my way home, I ran into my cousin Corey, who had already heard what happened, and asked if I was okay. He clued me in that he had seen Keisha's face: "I saw her face. You scratched the whole side of her face up, and she and about two carloads of her friends are on their way to your house to beat your ass." I thanked my 'cuz for the warning and immediately headed for my mother's house because I knew these bitches might run up on me. And the one thing I can say about Bridgette is, "She is not to be fucked with, period." (My mother had actually liked Kevin in the beginning, until he became a pretentious drug dealer who started putting his hands on her daughter.)

By the time I got to my mother's house, I found out that Kevin had already taken Keisha to the courthouse to press assault charges against me. I was stunned, hurt, and embarrassed; Bridgette, on the other hand, was livid and was not having any of it. Due to my grandfather Kenneth Williams, Jr. becoming a self-made millionaire, he held a lot of sway in our community; that pertained to his children too. The next day Bridgette called the State Attorney's office and spoke to them with a proposed resolution: If my mother relocates me (Bella) out of the state immediately, then the DA will drop the charges if I don't set foot back in the state. The State Attorney's Office agreed to it, so I immediately flew to Fort Worth, Texas, to stay with my cousin Cynthia, who was in the Marines. I was there for about two months. However, I wasn't feeling it there, and I moved back to New Jersey. As long as I stayed away from Kevin, I was good.

In 1995, my mother married my stepfather, Robert Thomas, whom she had been dating for about 2 years. And he moved into the house where we were all living, including my Granny who had relocated to New Jersey after she retired. My stepfather Robert was a very nice, outgoing guy with brown skin, a short fade haircut, and a beard/goatee; he was short at 5'8" and a little on the heavy side at about 240 pounds.

I met Robert Thomas when I was 21, so I was grown; not being raised with him, I didn't have the same feelings for him as my brothers. Bridgette would say she's glad because if I were a teenager, he probably wouldn't have been around. I was snappy 'and mean.' — No man was going to come in here and tell me what to do because my own father wasn't even here, so my mother knew that if she tried to send a 'copy of a father,' there would have been a problem. I would have won. Luckily for all of them, I was grown.

Now, my brothers called my stepfather 'father.' I don't call anyone 'father.' Were the brothers close to their stepfather? Was he good to the brothers? He was a great man. Not till many years later, when Granny passed, my mother really started embellishing the truth—meaning she was 'a liar'—and we would just be nice and say, "Bridgette is *embellishing*." But when my mother and I got into it, Robert would kind of take her side, which he was supposed to, and I have no problem with that.

But before my grandmother died, my mother and my stepfather were having problems, and while they worked it out, Robert was going to move into his own apartment, which was closer to his job across the bridge. My mother and stepfather had a meeting with all of us to let us know what was happening. And I was vociferous, "Well, I'm not staying here; I'm moving in with Robert (my stepfather)," and they were kind of laughing, and then my brothers said, "We don't want to stay here either." Then the two of them kind of worked it out, but I told them straight out, "Y'all ain't gonna get me stuck here with all of them."

The mortgage was the number one concern because if Robert left, that would leave Bridgette and Granny paying the mortgage. If I had moved in with my stepfather, he would have let me buy a Lamborghini and even co-sign for it! HA! Robert would let me do anything. If I'd gone with him, I'd have a ball. He would say, "Oh sure, I'd sign for you, Bella, because I know you're gonna pay your bills." "Uh-uh," I said, "If he's leaving, I'm going with him." I had crossed over to the other side and told my mom, "I'm going with my stepfather!"

Robert was very kind and very nice; matter of fact, when I bought my Honda Accord—Granny had to co-sign because I didn't have the credit. And I wanted some rims and I wanted them *now,* not when I got paid, I asked my mother if I could borrow a thousand dollars and she said, "No!" I went to my stepfather, and he said, "Sure." And I paid him back in two weeks...so, I was 23 when I started working at the prison when I got my first car. Granny had taught us about credit but I had none at the time, so that's why she co-signed for me and that's how I started establishing credit because I paid my car off early too.

My stepfather worked as a Sargent in the New Jersey Department of Corrections for years; after marrying my mother he would eventually move up to Lieutenant in the rankings and retire. But my stepfather was also instrumental in the next course of my employment. Robert recommended I apply for a position at the New Jersey Department of Corrections. In his words, "You definitely have the mentality to do this kind of work, that is, "I don't give a fuck." Plus by now I had been hanging out with my cousins and friends who were in and out of jail.

Well, I passed the written and physical tests. And I completed my Police and Correction Training at the New Jersey Correctional System. Now, I am officially a Correctional Officer at the New Jersey Department of Corrections Annex. This prison held women that have been sentenced with a minimum of 2 years up to life with no parole. That sober meaning is, "They will never leave the prison, only in a pine box when they die."

At 5'3 and 130 pounds, it's true I was very petite but also true 'I have no fear of anything.' My first day was relatively quiet because the night before there was an altercation between two inmates who were dating and broke up. Their vehement argument turned intensely violent when one woman heated up a Tupperware container filled with hot water and threw it in her girlfriend's face, giving her second and third-degree burns on her entire face and neck area. The woman would stay in the burn unit for 3 solid months.

The following day our shift did a shakedown on the lockdown unit and found eight cellphones, marijuana, four shanks/makeshift knives, and two dildoes made from tape and socks. About a month later I came upon an inmate who became violently ill, throwing up and shaking—sweat dripping off her face. I attempted to take her to the infirmary. But Sergeant Lassiter stopped me in my tracks, letting me know the inmate was "dope sick" - no need for the infirmary. That woman would stay right in her cell and deal with her "withdrawal symptoms" on her own. It's sad to say but 80 percent of the new inmates coming into the system were between the ages of 18-25 and they were all "dope sick." Bella got her eyes opened *big time*– "Welcome to the World of Incarcerated Women."

On the weekends, I was never really into the party scene like my friends. I would stay home and spend the entire weekend reading a 300–400-page book while my friends hung out at the clubs. My favorite authors were James Patterson, Tom Clancy, and Dean R. Koontz. This is truly a family tradition I'm continuing. These were the books that my mother and grandmother read; we always made sure we had plenty of books in our home.

One day I was hanging out at my best friend Cheyenne's house and decided to go to the liquor store for her while she was getting ready for a night out. As soon as I pulled up to the liquor store, I saw my *ex*-boyfriend Kevin standing outside with my cousin. I hadn't seen him in a few years, but that damn man always gave me butterflies whenever I saw him. He was six feet tall, dark, and handsome but 'wasn't shit.' Our eyes made contact and we said hello without incident, and the next thing I knew his girlfriend jumped out of the car and started screaming and staring us down.

Suddenly, she walks up to me and takes a swing. She misses my face and hits my ear, knocking my earring to the ground. I'm in shell shock for a few seconds. I turn to look at Kevin and my cousin Marcus and I remember hearing one of them say, "You better hit her back." I look up at Keisha. She is crying and walking away. I immediately process this—somewhere along the line, I have gained some wisdom. "I'm on probation for ninety days as a Correctional Officer and I am making twenty-six thousand dollars a year plus unlimited overtime..." With my renewed perspective, my eyes go from Kevin to Keisha to Marcus. *Nobody* has a job but me; it's not worth it.

At that moment, I turn, get in the car—never look back and head for my mother's house. When I arrive, I give her an instant replay of what just happened. The next day Bridgette instructed me to go to the Courthouse and press charges against Keisha. I did, but within a week I found myself sitting down with my Granny. I told her unequivocally, "I am dropping the assault charges against Keisha. I know what it is to love that man, and I am not going to allow her to end up with a record because of him- he isn't worth it." I reiterated to Granny, "*I am dropping the charges.*" Granny paused and told me with great genuineness, "Bella, I am *so* proud of you." Bridgette on the other hand was livid.

Later that year, I embarked upon another huge milestone in my life. For the first time, I met my biological father Michael Daniel St Patrick in person. It was not, however, a social visit. My father drove up from Tallahassee, Florida because, Yvette Jackson, his twenty-seven-year-old daughter, and my half-sister, was dying of alcoholism. I have two half-sisters through my father. I had met both the sisters when I relocated to New Jersey, but never really hung out with them. Yvette Jackson was the oldest at 27; she lived in Trenton, New Jersey which was about 45 minutes from me, and then there was Makiya Brown who was 25. She lived about 15 minutes away. I have to give it to my father, if he did nothing else, he made some beautiful daughters. (To be fair, my father Michael is a very handsome man—beautiful brown skin, 6'1," on the thin side, about 165 pounds. I understand my mother's attraction- I'll give her that.)

That night my father decided to take all his daughters to dinner at *On the Bay Seafood Restaurant* in South Orange, New Jersey. Mikaya the middle daughter declined the invitation; she has never spoken to our father, Michael St. Patrick, and has no desire to. Michael was never a part of any of our lives, so I understood her feelings completely. But when I found out later in life that my father's mother had died in childbirth—giving birth to him—the abandonment issues began to make sense to me. Perhaps, not having the love of a mother made him not care about having anything to do with his own daughters. He…like me…couldn't afford to get close to anyone. (I didn't get much from him…but probably inherited that trait.)

Whatever our sad history, that evening Michael our father, and his daughters, Yvette and I, thoroughly enjoyed our dinner. They both had the famous Crab cakes and I ordered the Crab Imperial which I adore—that and Lobster Thermidor are my favorite seafood dishes. (I must give credit when it's due and my mother makes the best Lobster Thermidor ever.)

After dinner, we stopped by the liquor store on the way to my Uncle Theodore's house where my father was staying. The Crown and Keg Liquor store was the most popular one in town. My father bought my sister Yvette a gallon of Seagram's Gin and two lemons. That night I got my 'virgin' introduction to a drink Yvette called, "Lemon Drops." Now, there was a special way to imbibe this drink. First, we would drink the gin straight from the glasses; then, you would pour salt on a slice of lemon and suck on it. *This* was your "Lemon Drops." That was my first time having that drink, but I wouldn't be a virgin for long…it surely wouldn't be my last.

Yvette explained to me she had been an alcoholic for about 6 years. She in fact was on disability as she wasn't able to go to work because she couldn't get out of bed without having a drink first, AND she was dying from it. I was so confused. Here was this tiny, beautiful woman in whom I saw no signs of alcoholism, but her kidneys were shutting down and about two weeks later, she passed at the age of 27. Thankfully or not, she had no kids. This whole thing was overwhelming. The same year my stepfather Robert lost his daughter Jordan due to excessive menstrual bleeding. She was left in the River Oaks Hospital lobby for nine hours and seemingly forgotten; she had no kids either.

Uh-*Mayberry* was a real dose of *reality*; it was "no joke." In the scheme of things, I do try to see all sides, I really do—The Good, the Bad…and 'The Ugly' was to come… I graduated high school, came home, dove into the deep end of the pool…and was still trying to keep my head above water.

Chapter 7

...and The Ugly... "Kevin and *Lemon Drops*"

Kevin Rhodes, my husband-to-be, was born on March 19, 1972, at 3:33 AM. No two ways about it, Kevin turned out to be fine as hell. He is a combination of Denzel Washington and Idris Elba. He has the ideal height at 6'1 and 220 lbs. of pure muscle. Add to that flawless, chocolate-colored skin, a bright beautiful smile, and flashing eyes to match and your knees wobble. He keeps a short fade haircut with waves for days. He is bowlegged—on both legs—and walks with more confidence than any man I've ever seen. An intelligent man, he is equally charismatic, *and* a lover and a fighter. Hm-hmm. And while viewin' him closeup while sucking down my "Lemon Drops," (*guzzling, more accurate),* I see that picture of Denzel and Idris smilin' down on me in Kevin's face.

Though I completely understood why my mother hated Kevin—the man who beat my ass whenever he felt like it. "Yes," I admit, I agree with her, and yet, "I stayed with him for years, thinking this was normal behavior."—After all, where I live, is 'The Land of Beating Women.' All my friends as young adults were beaten by their boyfriends. Kevin would stay out all night with the excuse that he was "working"—when I say "working," I mean he was *'a pharmaceutical sales representative without the license—aka a crack cocaine drug dealer.'*

I vividly recall one night I was at my apartment that I shared with Kevin when I received a phone call from my best friend Cheyenne. It was September 1, 1993. It was a beautiful Fall night with brilliant red, yellow, and greenish-brown leaves resplendent on the trees just like my friend, Cheyenne Knight, who is drop-dead gorgeous. She stood 5'5", a perfect size10 and 140 pounds. Light skin with beautiful black hair, she had a glowing complexion with deep dimples on each cheek, and when she smiled straight white teeth greeted you. Damn perfection. Cheyenne never wore the same outfit or hairstyle twice. The lady was stunning and she knew it; she wasn't conceited but she was *definitely convinced.* Ha! All the men wanted her and every woman wanted to be her.

Cheyenne was super intelligent but not *too smart when it came to men*—none of us were at that age. She had two beautiful kids, a son and a daughter. Unfortunately, both of her kids' fathers died tragically when the kids were very young, so she was left to care for them on her own. Fortunately, she could count on the help of her family and friends. I helped whenever I could. I would take the kids out to eat and to the movies to give Cheyenne a break and some time to herself. She had a big family too, 3 sisters and 1 brother. Cheyenne's mom Rose was as beautiful as her name and Cheyenne looked just like her. I always remember that Rose treated me like a daughter from the first day I met her; she showed me nothing but love, kindness, and respect.

So, when my best, loyal friend Cheyenne called and said she had some important news to tell me, she had 110 percent of my attention. – She heard Kevin was with some woman at *Mr. Joe's Pool Hall*—hm, hmm—that's all it took. I immediately jumped into my 1991 4-door turquoise Blue Honda Accord. Now, this car is my baby and deserves a full description: My Honda Accord had silver specks throughout the paint job which caused it to shimmer in the sun. It had 17-inch chrome rims with a speaker in the back seat and my sunroof was often open blasting *Snoop Dogg Gin and Juice* as was the case this night as I drove straight to the pool hall in the proverbial *like a bat outa hell.* I loved that car and it loved me!

When I entered the pool hall that night, it was packed to the max. There were about fifty people having fun, laughing and enjoying themselves. This local, popular establishment had been open for years. It was even a hang-out spot for my parents back in the day. It was small and cozy but plenty was going on. It had ten pool tables in the back and in the front there was a little kitchen where Ms. Wanda cooked up their signature dish, "Cheesesteak and French fries." They were so delicious! To this day, I can taste the seasonings—succulent meat, fried onions, and melted cheese with every bite. This legendary sandwich doubled the meat of the average sub, and the French fries were exceptionally crispy and soft on the inside. It was worth every bit of the ten dollars they charged!

Enticing aromas aside, it didn't take long for me to zoom in on Kevin's tall chocolate-fine ass and I headed straight for it. Of course, there were 3 or 4 women just buzzin' around him like queen bees (so they wished), grinning up at him adoringly and battin' their damn eyes. I approached him; I was calm…for the moment and said, "So what's going on? I heard you were up here with your *'other girlfriend.'* Which one is it?" Kevin started laughing in my face like I just cracked a joke. Now, he's just playing right in my face, so I raised my voice authoritatively, "Which one of these *'hoes'* are you fucking?"

Mind you, I am 5 '3, 130 pounds, and smaller than anyone in the building but I could care less about that! So, Kevin just flicks me off like a fly, "Take your dumb ass home. I'll talk to you later." Well, of course, that didn't go down well, as I stood my ground and replied cockily, "I'm not going anywhere."

Without missing a beat, Kevin leans in and immediately smacks me so hard with the back of his hand that I instantly fall to the ground. And if that wasn't bad enough, here comes the real humiliation: Before I can get to my feet, Kevin grabs me by my hair and drags me out of the Pool Hall—in front of all those people—and continues to drag my ass outside—all the way to my car where he drops me to the ground and repeats, "I told you to take your dumb ass home." At that point, I was so defeated; I just did what he said. They were all frightened of him—everyone in that building—90 % of the men in the town feared him; he was a beast with actual boxing skills. I cried myself to sleep that night. It was around 2:00 AM and Kevin still wasn't home. I knew then this man could not love me and treat me this way; he would never be faithful to me because he truly belonged to the streets. It was a week before my head finally stopped throbbing from the pressure of him dragging me by my hair across the parking lot.

One of the many times Kevin was released from prison, I set up a meeting with a semi-famous Boxing Coach, Barney the Brutal, from Uppercut Boxing Gym in West Orange, New Jersey. The day of the meeting Kevin left that morning and promised he would be back in time. He wasn't, instead, he went to make a drug run to New York. Naturally, I was pissed and laid his ass out when he nonchalantly walked in. His wise-ass response was, "I would rather sell crack to Mike Tyson than fight him. There's more money in it." He laughed and walked away like he really said some profound shit.

There was another night deep in my memory that stands out. Kevin was supposed to be home and I was hovering over that clock like a hen giving birth. Every minute that passed infuriated me more; it was like another dagger penetrating my heart. Well, I didn't have any scissors in the house but I got this brilliant idea—or so I thought—to avenge his sorry ass.

– Kevin *loved his shoes.* He easily had 48 pairs of tennis shoes. So, I took a seat on the floor...accompanied by a 'steak knife'(because there wasn't a pair of scissors to be found) and cut every single shoe. I was damn proud of my accomplishment, 48 pairs x 2 = 96 ways to piss him off! And what earth-shattering thing happened when the man got home?? He looked at them all and said, "All you had to do was cut one of 'em up and it would have ruined *a pair.*" Laughingly, he didn't even give his mound of serrated shoes a second look. He wasn't even mad; he just made me look stupid—"You only had to cut one shoe from each pair, and you sat here and cut each shoe, you dummy..." So much for vengeance. That's the kind of relationship Kevin and I had—$3,000 worth of shoes annihilated, no problem. He had so much money from drug dealing,' that he didn't care. This wasn't collateral damage, just another reason to buy more shoes.

So WHY would I continue to stay with him?? Please know that Kevin and I had our good times too—the thorns *and* the roses. Though the thorns stayed forever and the roses died quickly, they were beautiful while they lasted. I especially remember my birthday weekend of June 10th. Kevin took me to the Poconos in Pennsylvania. It was a beautiful room with a very romantic, heart-shaped bed, the kind the resort is specifically known for and is a draw for all the couples. There was even a champagne-shaped jacuzzi in the room! It was the most amorous, charming accommodation I had ever experienced.

On our first night, Kevin took me to a gorgeous restaurant on the water's edge. The water was still and reflecting the moon above it. We feasted on lobster tails dipped in warm butter, perfectly steamed asparagus with herbed butter, and baby potatoes, nicely seasoned. The meal was scrumptious and the lobster was so decadent! (My Granny set the standards early as I was growing up. With her ever-fresh garden and her high caliber of cooking, I always had a great appreciation for a fine-cooked meal; even the vegetables had to be cooked and seasoned properly.) Here, the asparagus had just enough crunch on the outside and was soft and succulent on the inside; the potatoes were so creamy and the texture so silken, they almost melted in my mouth and it did not end there. For the showstopper dessert, we had their famous "Lemon Blackberry Souffle"; it was magnificent! We finished off with two Pepsis, a regular for Kevin, and a diet for me. I sent *kudos* to the Chef that night. Everything was superb!

And that was just the beginning of a grand evening. Following that masterpiece dinner, it was off to the casino where we played for about 3 hours. It was great fun even though Kevin and I are not really gamblers. We won; we lost and ended up leaving with about two hundred dollars in our pockets. Then we casually walked back to the room, hand-in-hand, watched some TV, made beautiful love, and fell into a delicious sleep. Saturday, we went to a rock and roll music festival that was taking place nearby, and then we spent the rest of the day at the Water Park. I thoroughly enjoyed myself. We had no arguments; there were no indiscretions at all on his part. Honestly, it was one of the fondest memories I've had with Kevin.

Sunday morning, we had a fantastic brunch at the French Quarter Restaurant. The decor was exquisite; inside the restaurant, it had cathedral ceilings decorated with paintings just like you would find in the Sistine Chapel. Kevin had the breakfast crepe which consisted of eggs, ham, bacon, and cheddar cheese nestled in a special crepe, and served with a glass of freshly squeezed orange juice. I had the "French Strawberry-Cheesecake Crepe" which featured sweetened cream cheese, and freshly cut strawberries from the summer season. After brunch, we returned to our room, packed our bags, and headed home. ...Sometimes, going home can also be fun because now you are filled from top to bottom with all the fine memories you experienced in your romantic weekend hideaway.

...*However*, it didn't take Kevin long before the man went back to his old ways. (It seems like one good weekend is supposed to make up for the other 360 days of abuse.) Kevin's routine is to have breakfast with me which comes from a wide array of foods and choices: the likes of bacon, sausage, scrapple, steak and eggs, omelets to waffles, French toast or pancakes, crepes and eggs benedict. Not all at the same time, of course, but breakfast is our favorite meal. So, like I said, Kevin starts the day eating breakfast with me, and then he usually leaves at about 11 AM to go to work. "Work" consists of going *'To the block/streets selling crack cocaine to the crackheads.'* I am actually doing something positive for myself—enrolled in school and taking computer specialist classes at Berkeley Community College.

By the time I get home at 6:00 PM, Kevin will have my dinner ready...yes, he did... The man was not only fine but he did 95% of the cooking. (I told you there were "things" I liked about him.) If you recall, I never had an interest in learning how to cook. With my Granny, my mom, my aunts, and even my youngest brother taking over the kitchen and doin' all the cooking, it's like they say, "There are too many cooks in the kitchen." After we eat dinner, Kevin is off to the streets again...doing *'more work—or pleasure,'* and I see him normally around 2:00/3:00 AM when he ends his day.

This particular day was a Saturday, so no school for me on the weekend. I awoke around 9:00 AM. There is no Kevin in sight. I immediately grab my cell phone and call him; it just rings and there is no answer. I am more pissed than anything because in my heart I know he is fine, nothing's wrong; he is out being the dog that he is. About 10:30 he strolls in the apartment grinning, gold teeth glimmering in the sunlight. I say, "Where have you been?" I get the brush-off answer from him, "Don't worry about it, fix me some breakfast." I answered just as flippantly, "Fuck you, you get whatever bitch you stayed with to fix you breakfast." Kevin looks at me and starts laughing and walks out, just like that. Of course, my dumb ass calls him, and he doesn't answer. And I call, and call, and, finally after the tenth time of calling with no answer, I give up.

Kevin never came home that night. I couldn't sleep. I tossed and turned in the bed and had horrible dreams—maybe he was hurt in a car accident, and then I would wake up and get mad all over again. He could at least answer the damn cell phone so I can know he is all right. I must have finally drifted off to sleep because when I woke up it was about 10:30 AM and Kevin was looming over me at the top of the bed ordering me, "Get up and fix some breakfast." And do you know what my dumbass did? I got up, washed my face, brushed my teeth, and fixed him breakfast without asking any questions about his whereabouts in the past 24 hours. So, you see, it wasn't just the physical abuse; it was also the mental abuse, and honestly, that was the worst. That's when I truly knew I was broken. I accepted whatever he did to me. I had no self-love, only love for him and he used it to his complete advantage. Kevin was in and out of jail in the next few years and I was just trying to make my *own* way in muddy waters…

In 1995, I worked for the State of New Jersey Treasury Department for the tax season and then decided to try something I'd never tried before. I had my first lesbian encounter. Her name was Mya Cummings; she was the supervisor, a tiny thing about 5'5", 115

pounds, light skin with a boy cut, giving a sexy stud tease. Tell you what, I was intrigued and very much down with it. Mya and I dated for about 4 months before I found out she had a girlfriend—*the whole time I was with her*—and I was over it then. I've only been in love one time so you're not goin' to play those games with me. If I'm not in love with you; – I can just cut you off...real quick. - I was done with that. Men, Women, lies, disloyalty...I gotta do something just for me, period.

So, I did. In 1999, as a smart, independent, enterprising 25-year-old, I moved from my family home and had a three-bedroom house built on an acre of land from the ground up. It was about 45 minutes away in Maplewood, New Jersey. I decided that by moving to Maplewood I would make ***'my dream'*** come true. *"I will get married, have kids, join the PTA, and raise a family, loving my children and husband."* Good, solid intention! I meant it.

Now, this was a very "big deal"—I am the only granddaughter amongst three grandsons, and "*I am*" the first to build my own house—a huge "milestone!" Well, what happened is—my colleagues where I worked at the jail, were always poking fun at me on how good I was at paying bills. When I was looking for an apartment to rent, they started telling me, "No, you should buy a home." So, I went to Granny and announced, "Hey I'm going to buy myself a home." My grandmother and mom came with me when I went to apply for the mortgage; it was a package deal—the house and the land were $91,000. -My Credit Score at the time was about 760 and the loan officer said, "This is very impressive for"-- she caught herself, she almost said, —for a Black woman....but said instead, "I have never seen a woman with credit so great at your age." I was so proud of myself; I *was only 24 years old* and buying a house of my own. It was awesome; there was a lot of paperwork to fill out so it took a few months to complete. Granny and my mom said, "Oh, they don't even give homes to married people, but it's a good experience...[for you to go through the process]."

Well, lo and behold, I called the loan people to check on the status and they said, "You're approved." So, it began, my brand-new adventure though I couldn't afford to live in the county in which my mother lived; I lived in the poorest county. My house was on ¾ of an acre, a 3-bedroom home with a chandelier and many other items in a $91,000 package. The same house in my mother's county would have cost $220,000. Laughing, "No one was giving me a loan for that, so I had to move where I could afford." But I learned a big lesson at a young age: If you're going to buy a home, it's better to buy the smallest house in a better zip code where you can build on it and it can make money for you, versus having the 'biggest house in the worst neighborhood,' where your resale value is still going to be the same because the location is not as good.

As no one in my family had ever had a home built, we literally had a meeting in the model home where we were given a book to choose all the design options. There was a book for the countertops, a book for the chandelier, and one for the carpeting—we had to pick out everything; it was pretty cool. It was me, my mother, and my grandmother pouring over all the choices. Just relying on me, I hadn't a clue, so we would all decide together. My aunts, Jacqueline and Joan, weren't there. But Aunt Jacqueline the classy one explained to me—as I had chosen blue carpeting to match my floors—she said, "Always go with a neutral color like beige because it could go with any color scheme," so I learned.

It's weird, my childhood also prepared me for one aspect of being a homeowner! When I was a little girl, we had lots of mice in the wintertime. My mother and Granny were terrified of mice. I on the other hand feared nothing; every time we heard the mouse trap snap, killing the mouse, I had no problem throwing them out. So, my Indiana childhood prepared me for major mouse patrol. When I built my home, the neighborhood had many open fields; in October, November, December, and January, I would probably chuck out twenty mice a month. That didn't scare me in the least

What *did scare me* was something else... This new housing development was quiet and peaceful. The problem was—it was *"too quiet and peaceful."* Going from my family home, comprised of my mother, stepfather, Granny, and two brothers, to "home alone" was not a good recipe. In no time, I became depressed, and being a 'total homebody,' it didn't take long for me to pick up a bad habit. *A very bad habit*—I started drinking—and yes, it was Seagram's Gin just like my sister Yvette drank...and eventually died from. But I rationalized...'That was her—not me.'

...Once I drank it that night, I decided to drink it again, I got bored and decided to drink; even if it was a good day at work, I decided to drink. As you can probably guess by now, it eventually became my daily routine. I'd probably drink for about 2 hours, watch TV, eat dinner and then go to sleep. I considered it like a man coming home and having a couple of beers every night. Then, it became routine. Every day it was like a job for me—20 years— just like retiring from a real job except there are no benefits. I never quit—oh no. I am not a quitter. I never called out of work, yet I drank every day...*every day.*

My sister had taught me the "correct steps." I observed her closely... (so I could carry on the generational tradition). She would cut the lemon open, and sprinkle salt on top of it. Then, she would drink the gin straight and then suck on the lemon and that's what you call a *"Lemon Drop."* But it reached the point where Bella didn't have the money for the bottle *and* the lemon, so Bella just started drinking the gin straight out of the bottle. (Granny used to scold me, "At least you could put it in a glass." "Why?" I would counter; it tastes better this way.")

Since it became routine, I had to think about this from a financial standpoint. I always think financially, so I'm going to buy half a gallon like they have in the restaurant, and that's more economically feasible. It lasts me for seven days. So, I did that for 20 years. I would continue to drink daily for the next twenty years of my life. Did you hear that?? For the NEXT TWENTY YEARS, I drank *"Gin and Lemon Drops."* It became my drink of choice and my constant companion. (I want to say—2 months before I went into Rehab in 2019, that restaurant-size half a gallon of straight gin that had lasted me 7 days, now only lasted me 2 days. The doctors told me, they didn't understand how I was living and focusing, having that much alcohol in my system.)

And all this time, throughout the *"Gin and Lemon Drop"* years, I kept in contact with Kevin; he was in and out of prison and had a son by Keisha. I found out what prison he was in and wrote to him. That *correspondence* would come to change my life more than I would ever know. Sometimes, on the weekends, I would visit my family but then other times I wouldn't see them for a couple of months. – Looking back, living in that big 'ole house all by myself, was I assuming 'I was still in Wish mode that I'm going to get married, have kids in this house, and go to the PTA??' …I don't know, I was still searching during these years, for what I don't know…but my soul was not content.

It was 2003 and I continued to work at the prison as a CO, Correction Officer. Here and there, I would go out with the two ladies I went through my training with Latonya Brown and Lisa Campbell. We had a lot in common and worked the same shift. On May 5th of that year, a fight ensued in the cafeteria. Latonya was the officer assigned to the kitchen. As I escorted a few stragglers to the cafeteria—within a few seconds—I noticed an argument starting up. Then a fight broke out with approximately 5 inmates involved. I immediately called for backup on my walkie-talkie as Officer Brown and I attempted to break up the brawl; however, it grew bigger and bigger. Within 6 minutes of the fight starting, it ended with two inmates suffering injuries—severe enough to be admitted to the hospital, and Officer Brown had been stabbed in the right eye with a homemade shank. Sad to find out Officer Brown would never return to work again; she became 90 percent legally blind in the right eye. She would go on medical disability and resign from her position. That situation never stopped haunting me. I think it was then I started thinking about my next career move. I had been there for seven years without being assaulted; I was very fortunate.

When I first started as a CO, I used to say, I could be around any kind of people and adapt to it, but I began realizing I can be in any environment and that environment adapts to me. Even though I was a petite little one, I learned all about the prison culture and knew, they're not just going to say anything to me—you respect me and I will respect you. – And I learned you had to act the same way every day. The worst thing you can do is—"Today, I'm happy, smiling and speaking to you and tomorrow don't talk to me, don't look at me." So, I kept it the same way one hundred percent, and I let them know, "I am not afraid to fight so don't get it twisted." Once you set your boundaries and stick by them, you're good. I didn't just work at the women's prison. There were about 15 prisons within a 10-mile radius, so whenever they had a riot, they would move us; I worked in men's prisons too.

Both the male and female inmates me a lot and they had a lot of respect for me. They gave me a lot of advice to keep me safe on and off the prison grounds, especially since I'm so small. For instance, if I'm outside on a street going to a Club—and maybe attacked by a man, they were saying, "You don't need to buy all this fancy stuff; don't waste your money on mace, just use the hairspray you have in your purse, and spray it in someone's face and run away, or use a rat-tooth comb or a pen to stick in someone's neck, and that way you can shock them enough so you can run.

But inside the prison, we had gear, and if it was a big issue, we had a riot team that would come in but normally it would just be us to break up the fight unless it got too big. – Unlike some people may think, you don't have weapons in the prison, you only have a walkie-talkie and a pair of handcuffs because in a prison it's basically 1 Correctional Officer per 95-100 women or men that you have to keep under control. You cannot have anything on your person that can be taken from you and used against you.

Let's say, I am in Maximum Security and something happens—my base pay was about $23,000 plus $5,000 for hazardous pay. Any law enforcement person gets this because you sign a contract when you start that in this type of environment, in this type of job, you might not make it home, and you sign papers to that effect. You don't ever want to be in a situation like this. For example, I'm on a tier with 95 inmates; they overtake me and start beating on me. I reach out, "Hey open up the door and let me in." They're not going to let me out. They would just rather contain the situation and lose one Correction Officer than open that door and allow all the inmates to storm out. That's what we signed up for, and it makes sense because they'd rather have one casualty than the inmates spreading out and taking over the entire prison. So, you sign the papers saying you agree with this. – It's Law Enforcement. You're around murderers. – And it's so weird, we went to school at the Police and Correctional Training, so we did go to school with the police. For the first thirty days, we are together, and then we separated when they did their physical training and we do ours. And I remember talking to them about working in a prison around prisoners 24-7 and I said, "At least I know where 'the prisoners' are, you [the police] run into a house at 2 o'clock in the morning and you don't know who and what is lurking behind those doors." Hands down the future officers responded, "I will take my chances on the streets." They could not be locked in with prisoners 24/7.

Inmates taught me a lot and they had a great deal of respect for me, for the simple fact I gave them respect. It's always been like that; as long as you have a rapport with them, you can control it. But when you can't, that's when it blows up; it blows up very badly. That's pretty much how every prison in the United States is set up—1 officer for a hundred inmates and that's way too much. You can't control that. You just hope everyday things works out and you go home safe on your shift; that's all you can do when you work in that type of environment. Firefighters, Police, and EMTs (Emergency Medical Technicians)—you're going to help someone; you don't know who's in that environment. Is somebody sick or shot? You don't know what you're walking into. It's deep.

It's a very different mentality with the women and the men. For women, they assault each other and you remember the one that threw boiling water at her girlfriend's face. Now, for men, they usually use knives, or shanks—which women use too, but they don't just use a knife to stab someone with. What the men would do is defecate in the toilet and stick the knife in the poop. That way when they stab you, if the cut doesn't take you out, hopefully, the infection will kill you. If you're dead, they don't have to worry about looking over their shoulder anxious that they're going to come back and retaliate. So, when you do fight, "you fight to death."

Now, in prison TV shows and films, you're thinking inmates are just locked in their cells all day long. No. That's like a comic book. The Maximum-Security section is one part where they're locked down. The rest of the inmates— they go to school; they go to work; they go to the kitchen to cook—so the inmates are constantly moving around the prison yard. I remember my Mother saying, I remember my Mother saying, "Oh my God—if you go there tomorrow and feel like you can't do it? You can quit and no one's going to have a problem with it." I said, "Ma, I'm tough, I'm not worried about anything." Most of my relatives were in and out of jail, I didn't even know who they were—but I met them when I moved back here to New Jersey. Life is strange, 'You are where you are for a reason…and you don't even know it, but it's preparing me for my job "in" prison.

Let's be very clear, the inmates run the prison, they just allow the CO's (Corrections Officers) to come in and do their jobs. You can't control that type of environment. You just hope everyday things works out so that you go home safe after your shift; that's all you can do when you work in that type of environment.

Also, just so you know, "Everyone who goes to prison, is not just another derelict or wine-o on the street. You have lawyers; you have judges; you have beauticians; you have scientists; you have chefs. All types of people are in there."

In prison you have women with all types of skills. Some of the women have the most gorgeous, healthiest hair I have ever seen in my life, prettier than the hair of most of the celebrities you see at the

Grammys or any award show. And that is because there are a lot of beauticians, barbers and make-up artists who have been convicted of a crime and are trading their skills; prison is very transactional. People have the misconception that prisoners are all poor, homeless, and throw-away people, when in fact it is the complete opposite. You have doctors that have committed and were convicted of crimes that were not considered "blue collar crimes" and ended up in state prisons. White collar criminals do not go to State prisons. They do their time in a nice country club setting, ha—a Martha Stewart type place.

And I don't think I could ever work with the criminally insane because even though people don't believe it, the more you're around someone, you start to take up their habits. You really do … and that's why they say, "Criminals go to prison to become better criminals," because they learn from their mistakes and other's mistakes. And the criminally insane may be cutting on themselves, I could either deal with the 'crazy' or 'convicted felons' but not both. So, I learned all about prison culture, and lived and worked right in the midst for 8 years.

The only reason I resigned is because there was a new element starting to develop: Teenagers started coming to prison with double-life sentences. They had absolutely nothing to lose, because they were never going home, unless in a pine box—meaning they are there until they die. This came with a new since of rage and resentment that was directed at the correctional officers. So, the assaults nearly tripled. It takes a few years for the inmates to finally come to terms that they are never leaving. At this point they realize this is their home and they try to make the best of it. A lot of the inmates have jobs that not only occupy their idle time, but also are a way to make money. When I say money, you made $3 an hour. Believe me back then, those were the "good jobs."

After a while, some adapt to their environment: they have religious services; they have fun creating and performing plays; they have singing groups; they have competitions; they also work; they can send money home or receive it, and they have phone call privileges.

The women there make it the best way they know how. They have access to therapists, along with the Infirmary, which is where inmates go when they are sick and need to see a physician or nurse. Like I stated before, when I felt that the inmate was so sick I attempted to take her to the infirmary, but I was denied by my Sergeant who informed me, "She is just dope-sick; take her back to her cell. She will go through her withdrawals there." Unfortunately, a lot of the inmates coming into prison are addicted to drugs and alcohol and will go through the same withdrawal process.

I believe I was 32 at the time, and I said, "This would be the time; either I'm going to do 12 more years as a CO to give me 20 years, or I get out now and go back to school. I chose to go back to school." It was an Adult Education course with Maplewood Adult Education Program. I enrolled in a nine-month program for Medical Billing and Medical Administration. And I resigned from the prison because of the amount of stress I was under. You automatically qualify for unemployment benefits because 'stress' is a major factor in Law Enforcement.

I completed the nine-month Medical Billing Program with a 95 percent average. I was *so* happy to start my new career. In 2005, after about 8 months of rejections from the predominantly Caucasian doctor offices I had sent applications to, I applied to and was hired by Dr. Chanigan Vinay as a Front Office Coordinator. He had three offices within his practice: One office was for primary care, one for cardiology, and then there was the specialist office that was comprised of Endocrinology, Nephrology, Infectious Disease, and Sports Medicine.

The primary care office was in Springfield, New Jersey, where I worked. I checked patients in and out, and scheduled appointments. There was only one other employee there at the time, Brooke; she had been there for a few years. We worked for two doctors, Dr. Rama Harpreet and Dr. Balakrishnan Patel. They were nice doctors. It was a very upscale Primary Care Office so we dealt with anything from sinus infections to a newly diagnosed cancer patient. Two weeks after I was hired, Brooke was fired for stealing Dr. Harpreet's prescription pad and writing Percocet prescriptions for her friends. She was terminated immediately, and I became the only employee.

The office manager Alex Miller sat me down and asked what I wanted to do. I was confused and said, "What do you mean?" Alex explained that if I was willing to stay, they would send someone down to help me until they could hire more staff (and replace Brooke). If I chose not to stay, he would just have to shut down the office. I was shocked; that was "a call to arms—*my arms*."

I answered him at once, "Hell no! - I got this; send me some help and we can rock this shit out!" Dr. Vinay, the owner, sent Melanie Griffin from his Billing Office to help. In the meantime, they interviewed for the two positions to be filled.

For the next three months, I was the Check-in, Check-out person and the Medical Assistant. I quickly moved up in the eyes of Dr. Vinay, the owner, and I was rewarded with a nice raise. I did not meet Dr. Vinay until about three months later, but when I did we immediately formed a bond. I didn't know it, at the time, but I would become one of, if not his favorite employee! Eventually, we had a full staff: Elizabeth Walker was a licensed Practitioner Nurse, and Roxi Raines was a Front Desk Coordinator.

The doctors would come and go when their 2-to-5-year contracts were up. They were all foreign doctors. Dr Chanigan Vinay, the owner, was born in Pakistan in 1933 and arrived in America in 1973. He and his colleague flipped a coin to decide if they would move to America or England; America won out. Dr Vinay relocated to Springfield, New Jersey where he had trouble being hired by any of his Caucasian colleagues. He started his career at the Emory Memorial Hospital in 1974, and within a year he had made his presence known. He was considered the best Cardiologist they had ever seen and was nicknamed GOD, because of his arrogance. Ha! Eventually, Dr. Vinay would open his own practice, and he vowed to hire only foreign doctors, so they would never have to experience what he did when he first came to America. (I liked him immensely and Dr. Vinay would become my biggest supporter.)

In 2007, Dr. Kiran Bhojani was the first female doctor to come on board. She was a primary care physician from Bangladesh: she was beautiful, and a little cocky. The first day I met her, I was late due to an appointment, so Elizabeth was there and opened the office for me. Dr. Kiran Bhojani and I pulled up in the parking lot at the same time. We introduced ourselves and started walking to the door. She arrived there first and paused. I didn't understand. I saw that she only had her purse in her hand so why did she stop? It didn't take long to figure it out; Dr. Bhojani was waiting for *me* to open the door for her. She had a rude awakening. We stood there for about two more minutes until she finally looked directly at me. I smiled back as pretty as I could while *she* opened that door. I knew then I was going to have a problem with her.

I continued to flourish at my job and I loved it. I remember one day I kept getting phone calls from patients enquiring about their blood test results. - I sent messages to Dr. Bhojani to follow up on the patient's blood work tests with callbacks to each of them. She never called them back, so I asked Elizabeth, the Nurse Practitioner, "Is Dr. Bhojani returning calls to your patients?" She responded, "Yes." I knew she'd give that answer because the two of them had grown very close since Dr. Bhojani had arrived. I came to work early a few times and they were having a meeting in her office. I didn't care about that; my issues were the patients being neglected and I was angry. I went into her office and asked her directly, "Why are you not calling the patients back?" She started laughing saying, "Bella, don't get upset; I was busy, I will call them later." I replied, "Okay," letting the issue rest for the moment.

But the next morning when I arrived at work, I received a call from Mr. Brian Jenkins, a patient who was extremely upset that he had not heard from Dr. Bhojani. He was very anxious about his test results. I found out 72 hours ago this patient had cancer because I had reviewed the test results and put them on Dr. Bhojani's desk for a callback. I apologized profusely to Mr. Jenkins and advised him I would have the doctor call him back today - I gave him my personal promise. I then went into an empty office and immediately phoned Dr. Vinay's office and told Natalie Roberts (Dr. Vinay's receptionist), to please get Dr. Vinay on the line. "I have a serious issue going on in this office."

I waited on the phone for about three minutes before he came on the line. I explained everything that was going on and Dr. Vinay asked that I give him one hour. He would call Dr. Kiran Bhojani and get this straightened out. He ended our conversation by saying, "I will call you back tomorrow." He hung up with no goodbye. I continued with the day as usual but when I returned from my lunch break, Dr. Bhojani was standing before me 'apologizing' and letting me know she had called all the patients back. I was happy to hear that and I accepted her apology.

The next day Dr. Vinay called me and asked if Dr. Bhojani had apologized. I answered, "Yes, she did," and he responded in a firm voice, "I told her if I get one more phone call from Bella I will move her out of that office and send her to the Primary/Specialist Office." I never had a problem with her after that. I remember relaying this story to Granny, and she laughed and said "Dr. Vinay must really care about you; he is ready to move a doctor out of the office for you. -- You must be really doing a great job there." "I am," I answered with a sense of pride, "and he continues to give me raises under the table!!" That was a very happy moment for both Granny and me. I was loving life, but my dating life sucked. I would date here and there but nothing was exciting or permanent. What else is new? My life was a continuous "upswing," and "downswing." I was happy and sad; I was complete in some things and empty as hell in others. Was I just getting used to this tempo as normal? Or was I learning to go with the flow of life…

Chapter 8

…The Loss of "My Rock" "Love Lands Me in Hell"

When I built my home at the ripe old age of 25, I wanted to make everything perfect. This was going to be the place where I would make my dreams come true. When selecting my furniture, I chose a beautiful color scheme of green and cream. My Granny loved to make Afghans, so she made this adorable little throw blanket that matched my furniture. The blanket was perfect for lounging on the couch and when you got a little chilly, you could throw the Afghan blanket on top of you and feel all cozy. I still have it…and always will. It's one of my prized possessions. (It has a special spot in my present apartment.) When people in our family were having babies, sweet Granny would make a pink ABC blankie for the girls and a blue ABC one for the boys. It would also feature the name of whoever was having the baby, so quite a few of our family members have treasured Afghans made by Granny's loving hands. None of us inherited the trait. - We didn't have the patience; nobody could sit still long enough, but all of us can remember sitting and watching Granny nimbly working her little needles crocheting all night long while she was watching TV. It became a familiar and comforting sight.

Once I went shopping with my Aunt Jacqueline—the one who

looked like a movie star and had such class and taste—and she spent four hundred dollars on one pan! Years later when I moved into my first apartment, I bought myself a 10-piece set of pots and pans for thirty-nine dollars and ninety-nine cents at Walmart, and I was just as happy. Jacqueline told me when she was growing up, she and her friends would go shopping at the mall; each would have $100 to spend. Her friends would spend their hundred bucks purchasing two or three outfits, while Aunt Jacqueline would buy *one* good pair of pants or a shirt; she felt that was a much better investment. Even as a young woman, Aunt Jacqueline knew the meaning of quality over quantity.

My Aunt Jacqueline had such an impact on my life. Remember, Jacqueline was a part of that American Airlines class action lawsuit brought on by the employees who suffered debilitating asthma and breathing problems because of chemicals products that were improperly used. The products used to clean the planes weren't allowed to dry properly and the employees inhaled the noxious fumes. Although my aunt did receive a settlement check from the Airlines, she did pass away due to complications which caused a fatal asthma attack. Aunt Jacqueline's friend from nursing school had become a doctor, and she had requested a Pulmonologist (lung specialist) from Georgetown one of the most prestigious hospitals on the East Coast to consult with her. She showed the family Jacqueline's X-rays. Those films looked like a gun range where the target was shot through with bullets. There was nothing but holes in her lungs. The doctor said she couldn't believe Aunt Jacqueline was still alive. Jacqueline was always a liver and doer.

Jacqueline lived in her apartment in Annapolis, so my mother would always call and check on her to make sure she was okay because we all get depressed at times and don't talk to each other, a family trait. It just so happens, I'm at work one day and I get a call from the police, "Is this Bella St. Patrick?" I answered, "Yes." The policeman's voice on the other end pauses and then says, "I'm here with Jacqueline Williams (another slight pause). She's deceased and your name is on a card beside her." After I retrieved my breath, I said,

"Sir, what happened?" He responded, "She had an asthma attack and was reaching for her asthma pump. The way she was laying, she couldn't reach it." I said immediately, "Let me give you my mother's phone number. She's her next of kin." The landlord knew Jacqueline and all about her condition, so if my mother couldn't get in touch with my aunt, she would contact the landlord, and he would knock on the door to check in on her. They've had to bust down the door before because they knew it could be a life-or-death situation.

My dear Aunt ended up dying from breathing in the lethal chemicals all those years. It was a big, multi-million dollar lawsuit that was settled in the '90s or 2000s. Aunt Jacqueline was receiving a check from them and she was already retired. Fortunately, she lived for some years with breathing diseases, but how long depends on the health of your immune system. It's like the mesothelioma in the mining camps. There is such dangerous stuff out there, sometimes that can't even be seen or smelled.

But while it lasted, it was nice having the whole family together in the New Jersey area, and even though I was 30 years old by then I was still learning new things about them. Once Granny told me a story that her mother—Lucille—would never allow all her kids to ride in the same car at the same time when they were going to the movies, (remember, there were 10 or 12 siblings in the family). Her brood of children would have to ride in separate cars because great-grandmother Lucille felt if you had an accident and all the kids were in the same vehicle, it would wipe out the entire family... Now, that I think about it, what car could have fit 12 kids back then?? I guess it's likened to the president and the vice president never flying in the same plane at the same time.

-It's ironic because years later, my grandmother, myself, and my cousin were riding in a car coming back from—I don't know where. There were 3 generations of us: Myra, my cousin was probably about 6 at the time, I was about 30, and my grandmother was probably in her 60s. I was driving; my grandmother was on the passenger side; and Myra was in the back seat. Suddenly, for some unexplained reason, the car just shuts off, and here we are starting to lose speed as we're cruising along Interstate 97—a busy four-lane highway. Instantly, I begin to veer the car to the right so I can access the shoulder, and I hear Granny's anxious voice shouting out, "What are you doing?" I responded immediately but calmly to avoid panic, "Granny, the car shut off." I was able to reach the shoulder fairly quickly. We sat there for a minute and then I proceeded to start the car. The engine responded and that familiar "starting sound" allowed all of us to exhale a sigh of relief. Soon, I could maneuver the car back onto the highway. I remember glancing over and seeing my grandmother praying intently. She raised her eyes to the heavens, "Oh my God, that would have been 3 generations taken out." ...That was a sobering thought.

I was able to make it home without further mishaps. The next day my grandmother went straight to the mechanic, told him what had happened, and expressed her urgent desire to get rid of the car. Granny decided to buy another car because she didn't want to take another chance with that one. Whatever the mechanic did with the car after that—Granny wasn't worried—it wasn't about the money. The car was paid for and she was not going to have "that catastrophe" on her conscience. The mechanic couldn't find out what was wrong with the car, but Granny didn't care and stood firm, "I don't want it. I'll sell it to you." It made me think about the story she told me when I was a child—how her mother didn't want the children altogether in one car. And eerily, for us, it would have wiped out 3 generations—my grandmother, the granddaughter, and Myra the great granddaughter, if we had gotten hit on that busy Interstate with the car shutting down like it did. I think Granny was prophetic, along with all the other qualities she possessed.

In 2007 my father, Michael Daniel St. Patrick, came for a visit to my new house. He stayed about two weeks...and I can safely say for the better part of that time, we remained inebriated—father and daughter who never spent a day together until I was 23, now just thick as thieves. It was me, swiggin' down "Gin and Lemon Drops;" he was drinking his Bud light beer and eating his potato chips. He loved any and every flavor or brand of potato chips. I drank my Seagram's

Gin straight out of the bottle. (Granny hated that. She used to say to me, "Can you at least put it in a glass?" I told her, "No, it tastes better straight out of the bottle.") I will say this about my father—he made the best deviled eggs with the perfect amount of paprika and dill relish: it had just enough bitterness. So, these are the memories my biological father and I made passing on this disgusting, deleterious trait of alcoholism—let's say it like it is—for I have no idea, how many generations there were.

It's true, that our father wasn't present in the lives of any of his daughters…but as I said I believe it was because of his mother dying in childbirth; therefore, he never had an attachment—to anyone. After her death, the children were shuffled between family members. His father was now saddled with '4 kids and no wife,' so it was hard on all of them. Relatives divvy up the children to raise. Have I given my father *a pass?* …I don't know, but I kind of understand and think I have a lot of him in me as I too can easily detach, "Okay, this is how it is; I'm on my own. I'll figure it out. I don't need anyone else." I remember my mom saying once, "I can't ever just move to another state and know no one." Well, I've done that many times to get the hell away. (After I got out of Rehab in 2019, I knew New Jersey was a trigger for me. I will never go back to New Jersey because *I know* I'll pick up a drink. I'll move to any state not knowing a soul and start all over, but not New Jersey. Mm-mm, not for me.)

My father was the same way; he left home and never looked back or went back. There's nothing to do when you live in a small town like he did. I believe my dad graduated high school and I believe he got into trouble so many times that the Judge finally gave him an ultimatum, "Either you go to jail, or you go to the Viet Nam war." Michael chose the Vietnam War. That's how my father got there. That's what really happened; they kicked him out of the state. My father was so rough and uncontrollable, that going to Viet Nam was the best thing for him because he would have ended up in jail regularly. "Thank you, Judge, because it could have been worse."

In 2008, I received the most perplexing, heart-wrenching news of my life. My Granny was diagnosed with first-stage liver cancer.

She was scheduled for a same-day surgery at the University of New Jersey Hospital. It was supposed to be an 'in-and-out procedure.' The surgery went well—or so we thought, but then the doctors 'sent Granny home,' and she started having complications—trouble breathing, and looking quite jaundiced. We called the ambulance at once, and for the next few months, my Granny had to remain in the hospital. It was a time of high alert for all of us. – Granny was the central pillar of our entire family and we had to make sure she was cared for every minute. We arranged our schedules so that a family member would be there with her at all times.

I was in my 30s at the time and honestly, it was rough going. I couldn't let emotions overtake me because I had responsibilities and I've always worked two jobs to fulfill my obligations. At 25, I was already a homeowner and had a mortgage. Working in Corrections or the Medical Field didn't bring in a huge amount of money. So, every other weekend for 9 years, I would supplement my income by caring for a young man who was challenged with 3 different afflictions: he was born blind, had Autism, and Cerebral Palsy. His name was Bryson and I would privately sit for him on alternate weekends.

He was the son of two African American deacons whose acquaintances I made at church. Bryson was a delight to be with; he was 11 or 12 and a very bright, joyful-spirited young man. Whenever I walked into the room and greeted him, I'd call out his name, "Hey, Bryson!" His whole face would light up and he'd start laughing because he instantly knows your voice; he knows your smell; he knows all about you—even how much he can get away with!

Bryson's parents were Deacons Samuel and Brenda Harris; they were a beautiful family. Samuel was a very handsome African American man about 5'9" and 180 pounds with creamy chocolate skin; he worked out daily and was in great physical shape. Samuel owned an award shop; he laughed telling me even when the economy is bad, businesses will still give out trophies and awards, so his shop was always thriving. His wife Brenda Harris was about 5'3" and weighed about 185 pounds. A short, chubby, light-skinned woman, with shoulder-length salt and pepper locs, she walked with an air of cockiness and confidence. And you knew when Brenda was entering the room because she was dressed in nothing but the best—I mean the very best: Chanel and Dior dresses and pantsuits, Louis Vuitton purses, Milano and Jimmy Choo shoes, and of course, her jewelry was the finest, Cartier diamonds and watches. She was the director of a nursing home called Comfort Cove, in Springfield, New Jersey, and she really enjoyed her job.

Samuel and Brenda Harris had three sons, Brady 30, Bryson 15, and Brent, the youngest at 13. Brady is about my height 5'0" and 110 pounds; he was a tiny young man with chocolate skin and short, curly, pretty brown hair. He was a high school teacher for about 5 years until he became sick with Lupus and had to resign. Brent, the baby, was light-skinned with braces, 5'5", and about 115 pounds; he was tiny, awkward, and definitely going through puberty. One day I would talk to him, and he sounded like a little girl; the next thing you know, his voice changed to the deep baritone of a Barry White—it was so cute.

Now Bryson, who I cared for, stood about 5'7" and weighed about 130 pounds; he had a light-skin complexion and reddish-brown hair; he was a very handsome young man. Bryson speaks in his own language. He is amazing. Once you walk/guide him to his chair in the kitchen—he had his favorite spoon—you'd put it in his hand and the bowl was right there; he would feel it and actually feed himself. When I took Bryson to the grocery store, he loved to push the cart down the aisles; he would laugh and smile the whole time. Of course, you would have to guide him because he is 100 percent blind, but he really enjoyed this simple maneuver. I also took him to McDonald's; the chicken nuggets and French fries were his favorites. I learned early by watching Bryson that the one thing that tickled him pink with laughter was hearing his parents yelling at his brothers. It's as if he knew they were in trouble, and that was so hilarious to him. It was such a blessing working with their family. They made me feel as though I was a part of the family and that is what I loved the most.

His parents, the Deacons, had faced and overcome other challenges. The mother told me they both smoked crack cocaine before they totally changed their lives around. She was doing drugs when she was pregnant with Bryson, and the doctors told her ahead of time Bryson would have Cerebral Palsy. If she had taken this particular medicine beforehand, it would have helped the condition. Well, every medicine they gave Bryson made him worse. I don't know if it was the medication that caused his blindness but he received a trust from the government from the time he was born, which he will receive for the rest of his life, due to the medical mistakes that were made by the doctors.

Usually, his parents would have little meals pre-made which you would just pop in a pan and cook and Bryson would be sure to eat it. A couple of times, I had to fix the food for him—I remember "twice" I prepared the food. I put it in his bowl; I placed his favorite spoon in the bowl and watched as he lifted the spoon to his mouth. Suddenly, he just took that bowl and threw it. I said, "What the hell??" His mother came home, and Bryson started howlin' and his mother started laughin.' I explained to her, "It's not his fault. I can't cook," and she answered, "Okay, we're going to try it again." I tried it another time. *After that,* she said, "I'm just going to go ahead and keep the food prepared." However, that's when our McDonald's visits began, so every other week, I would tell Bryson we're going to McDonalds, and he would associate that with the Chicken McNuggets and French fries, and he would go crazy. He knew—blind and all—good food versus bad.

Bryson went to New Jersey School for the Blind from about five years old to twenty-one when he was automatically released at age twenty-one. On Monday mornings, his parents would drive down to the College where the bus would pick up all the kids that lived on the eastern shore and it would take them to the New Jersey School for the Blind. The kids would stay there until Friday, and on Friday the parents would pick them up. Bless his heart, he never was really around his parents because they sent him to school, and at 21 he got kicked out, and they put him in a day program. They had never really been around the child his entire life yet he was always so happy and cheerful; he didn't know any difference.

I tried to trick him because he wouldn't listen to me in the beginning. It was so cool to hear his father come in and say, "Hey, cut that out!" and Bryson would start laughing. So, we conjured up a trick when I told his father, "He knows your voice." The father understood, "Gottcha." The next time I came, I recorded the father's voice and played it when Bryson started acting like a fool. The parents were at Church. It worked for one weekend. The next weekend when I played the tape, Bryson began laughing and screaming. I played it again, and he went off again. I said, "Aw, he knows it's not his father." We fooled him for one weekend but he was so smart he figured it out.

Bryson had been out of school for years, but every so often I would hear him say, "Up Down. Up, Down," as he moved his arms up and down. I figured that must be one of the exercises he was taught in school, and yet being out of school all those years, he was still remembering—he's still so intelligent even though he has so many 'challenges.' This was an amazing experience for me. He taught me humility; there's always someone else out there worse off than you. Bryson was such a blessing.

Every job—no matter what it is—I would take a learning lesson from it. Working for Bryson, I learned how to maneuver in my home as if I were blind. I memorized everything in my home, from the light switches to the microwave numbers, to the knobs on the stove. Anything I thought would be useful and other tasks like Juliette Lewis performed in the film, *The Other Sister*, where she plays an intellectually disabled daughter whose character had Down Syndrome. (I've always had a special place in my heart for these children with their sweet faces.) In the film, Juliette's character wants to become independent and live on her own. But her parents were afraid to let her do it. What Bryson taught me is that I should learn to become self-sufficient and learn the skills to function so that if I ever became blind, I wouldn't be put away in some institution. I wanted to be like Ray Charles and function *inside my house*.

On the weekends I wasn't working, I would drive up and visit Granny and sit with her at the hospital, no matter what. On the weekends that I was working and privately sitting for young Bryson, someone else from the family was always there with my grandmother the entire time she was in the hospital—and that was for 6 months. It was a journey from the moment she had the surgery and was 'sent home' and developed complications breathing and the ambulance took her to the local hospital where she stayed for several weeks. Then she got transferred to another hospital that was well-known nationally and she stayed there for an additional 3 months. Following that is when the doctor called the family in for a meeting with Granny's team of doctors and told us quite frankly that when she's coming home this time, she's coming home to die…

During this time, my Granny was aware of what was going on and I remember I was so distraught. Finally, I summoned the words from the deepest part of my heart and told her, "I can't make it in this world without you Granny." She looked at me with those loving eyes and calm, wise demeanor and said, "Bella you are a big girl now -- you will be just fine." I didn't know how I was going to do that. – My Granny had been the most important person in my life since the day I was born and the only person I could trust and lean on every day after that...she was "My Rock."

I remember seeing Granny that weekend; then, I went to work, and on the weekend, I worked my part-time job with Bryson. The following week, the doctors sent Granny home. I'm steeling myself and preparing my mind—*okay,* they've sent her home to hospice. My grandmother lived with my mom, and of course, they sent her home to hospice at my mom's house, because we weren't going to have Granny die in a hospital. We wanted her around family. Granny was a shell of herself, but there was one good thing that happened when she came home.

The night that she died, I couldn't stay awake—I stayed in the same bedroom as my grandmother—I was pretty exhausted from work. Granny was doing a lot of moving around in the hospital bed, so I finally got up and summoned my mom, addressing her half-asleep, "Ma, can you watch her tonight? Let me get some rest 'cause I'm too sleepy, and I'll watch her tomorrow night." I was *so* happy I did that. – Granny passed that night, and my Mom was in the room with her. I would have felt *so bad* if I had fallen asleep and she had passed alone without a family member consciously there with her. In retrospect, I think there was a reason I was *so tired;* my mother needed to be in that room. I was so at peace it happened that way. My Granny died on October 26, 2008; she was born in '31 so that made her 77. She passed the day before my mother's 56th birthday. It was a sad day. I will never be the same.

But my Granny lived a great life. She traveled all over the world; she did. You know she loved to travel, and my Aunt Jacqueline, the flight attendant, would sometimes get free airline tickets. My grandmother made good use of them. One of her favorite places to travel was Jerusalem—she went there two or three times. I have an actual cross that Granny brought back for me from Jerusalem which I cherish. She loved it there and one time she brought back Holy Water from her travels there; I didn't get any...but I sure could have used some! Granny also loved Hawaii and went there several times and even faraway places like Guam and Japan where she would visit her nieces and nephews who were stationed in the military in these exotic places. However, although we did many things together, Granny and I never traveled together. And the one thing she wanted me to do before she passed was to '*go out of the country*,' so that is my mission before I leave this Earth, I'm going to '*go out of the country*.' That would make my Granny very happy.

"Everyone" loved my grandmother. At her funeral, there were about 200 people in attendance honoring her. On her 75th birthday, my mom threw Granny a "75th Birthday Party." There were about 100 guests in attendance and about 25 of them wanted to speak and pay tributes to Granny. At the church, it was packed front to back. Everybody wanted to speak—many spoke for five minutes—relating how Granny had touched their hearts, how she was just a kind person, 'to everyone,' *period!* My Uncle, my father's brother, is a Jehovah's Witness. In their religion, you're not allowed to step inside a church. That man came to my Granny's funeral, and yes, he broke *whatever rule there was that you can't go into a church.* – He did that out of respect for my grandmother.

When my Granny died, we all sat at her funeral—and the tears poured—we were all crying. I was there, my middle brother Brandon was there, and my youngest brother Jayden had to sit in the pew behind us because there were so many people paying their respects. And I situated myself so *all* my brothers could hear me and announced from my soul, "We have lost our Granny and our mother. Life has changed." I told them all, and I hope they heard me, "Our world will never be the same," because I knew…it wouldn't.-

When Granny died, I was *already* out-of-control drinking. *Now*…I didn't even care if I drank myself to death. Kevin was comforting. (Yes, 'the man' was still in the picture—*in prison*—but still in the picture.) However, you can only be so much comfort from a phone in a jailhouse which you're not leaving until 2011. (Yes, when Granny died, he was in prison.) And it's sad because I remember my mother telling me after Granny died—she had told my mother that Kevin was going to be my downfall…and it hurt me to my soul. My Granny knew me. She knew it—and she was *absolutely right* because 'she knew' her children and her grandchildren. Granny knew we were back together but she died before Kevin came home (maybe that was a blessing). But I had to learn…BIG-TIME.

Kevin was released from prison on January 14th, 2011and moved in with me. Remember when I said a while back that I started corresponding with Kevin and my life would change forever? Well, this is a continuation, an elaboration, an explanation of that sentence. Let's just say, when two people are writing letters and are not in physical touch on a daily basis, things look 'rosier,' more philosophical as the inmate can spend hours in his cell reflecting—and maybe it was genuine—because I was hearing change, maybe even growth in Kevin's words and voice, and if I'm being brutally honest, I'm even acting like a couple, "We'll get through this together," so you see, I wasn't just working two jobs just to pay my mortgage and bills but also to send Kevin monies for his commissary.

So, when Kevin is released and moves in—it is the 'honeymoon stage.' Things are going great...for a hot minute. He gets a job, and a car, and as I said things are lookin' *all Rosy*. In fact, we were officially married on December 24, 2011. Look, he was my 1st love; we'd been together... off and on for 21 years, so why not 'tie the knot?' ...Who the f--- was I kidding? Myself, of course. Within a few weeks 'the fine-ass man' was out partying and hanging out with his friends—something he claimed in the prison—he no longer wanted (the bullshit turns my stomach). I knew then he was cheating again, but this time I was a complete vindictive alcoholic. I was going to make sure he was not going to cheat in peace, not if I had anything to do with it.—There was a massive storm brewing within me that I couldn't even see. It was invisible...but I sure felt its fury building inside...a powerful feeling I had never felt before.

Within a few months, I finally got the information I was searching for (the wife or girlfriend is always the last to know). Kevin had a 24-year-old girlfriend named Aaliyah living in the projects with her four kids—with four babies' daddies—he sure picked a winner. I remember it was a Saturday morning at about 9:00 AM; his cousin Jonathan had stayed the night and I was already up drinking my gin, watching TV, and enjoying myself. Kevin got up and announced that he and Jonathon needed to go take care of some business and he would be back in a few hours. I wasn't buying it, "No the fuck you won't or I'm going with you." Kevin laughed (the same 'ole repulsive response) and said, "No, you can't go." "Okay," I answered nonchalantly and started getting dressed just like them.

... He thought I was playing. Newsflash: I wasn't playing. They walked out of the house, and I walked right behind them and hopped my ass in the passenger seat, closed the door, and spoke as naturally as could be, "Let's roll." Jonathan was sitting in the back and slid back in his seat as he should have. *'He can't control his wife.'* Kevin's not laughing now and spits out, "Quit playing. I got to go." I continued to sit and drink my gin (trusty companion, always with me) and smoke my Newport. I ignored his damn macho attitude. I remained calm as a cucumber, and replied, "Turn the car on. I want to hear some music." Kevin looked at me like I was out of my mind; his voice grew strong, "Get the fuck out!" ...Honestly? It made me smile, because this man doesn't have a clue. I have crossed over from *sober to drunk* and from *Sanity to Insane*.

I looked at him and gave him the biggest smile...it was 'genuine.' Then I proceeded to put both of my knees up, strategically placing both of my feet on his windshield, and with all my might I kicked the living shit out of it—probably eight times with significant force—shattering the entire windshield into a thousand splintered pieces. The sounds of furious breaking glass were amplified in the small space. In response to their open-mouthed, horror-stricken faces, I spoke unruffled, "I guess nobody's going anywhere today." The car was quiet. I think to say they were in total shock is an understatement. This was the first time Kevin really saw me snap since he came home from prison; I don't think he knew until that day the *'the monster'* I could become fortified with my Seagram's.

I proceeded to get out of the car at the same natural pace I had entered it, walked back inside the house, casually sat on the couch and watched some more TV. I was thoroughly pleased with myself. It seemed like an hour had passed before Kevin and Jonathan came into the house—they looked a little intimidated. I loved it! Kevin said in a nice, calm voice "So what are we going to do with my car?" I answered in a tranquil tone that matched his, "I will call a glass company and have them fix it on Monday." Surprisingly...he was satisfied with the answer and within 20 minutes his friend Damien had come to pick up him and Jonathan. I asked no questions. By this time, I was *over* him and the disrespect. ...But Kevin wasn't *over* me, oh no.

Do you know the shape of that tornado in *The Wizard of OZ*? This massive, gyrating spiral where there is so much havoc and turmoil and being right in the throes of it, you are thrown all over the place as you spiral downwards? Well, for the first time in my life, I was headed for the dead bottom of it. Get ready for the ride, Bella; it goes straight to hell.

Oh, I remember "this day" like clockwork—like a date and day frozen in time—May 23rd, 2012. It was a Wednesday and Kevin's car was in the shop having work done, so he dropped me off to work at the doctor's office and was scheduled to pick me back up at 4:30 PM. However, at 10:30 AM, I received a call from my cousin Rachael informing me she just saw Kevin's girlfriend driving *my car.* What the fuck! I said, "Come get me now." I told the doctor in charge I had important business to take care of and I am leaving for the day. Rachael picked me up and we went hunting through the projects—anywhere and everywhere—we felt this hood rat would be, blasting *Lil Wayne Tha Carter IV 6 Foot 7 Foot.* I love that album. Whenever I need a mental break from the stress, I immediately turn on any Lil Wayne album and rock out to it. This was a perfect time for *Lil Wayne* to accompany us.

I hadn't called Kevin yet; I didn't want to alert him that I knew. After about two hours of cruising the projects and other known places, we had no clue where else to go, so I called Kevin and screamed into the phone, "I am going to fuck you and that bitch up—where the fuck is my car?" Kevin, true to his dumbass-self starts laughing and playing stupid saying, "I don't know what you're talking about." I warned Kevin, "If my car is not home in one hour, somebody's going to jail." And I meant that shit. What I didn't realize was, it would be "*me*" going to jail that night.

I went back to Rachael's house to calm down because by then I was runnin' on some kinda high 'ghetto hood shit,' and I needed to get it together because this was not who I am. But I told Rachael, *sista to sista,* that I had these recurring dreams that I killed Kevin and I was 'okay with it.' I had already figured this out in my head. I would end up going to the prison where I previously worked—the New Jersey Correctional Center For Women—the only women's prison in New Jersey, which meant I would serve my entire sentence in protective custody or be sent to another women's prison out-of-state where I would be placed into the general population. I never had a problem fighting to protect myself, so if I had a choice I would prefer going 'out-of-state.' I definitely didn't want to be in protective custody. Fuck that.

After hearing the ferocity of my dream and its consequences, Rachael was a little taken aback and acted like she was afraid to take me home. I think after hearing the tale about my sobering dream and knowing me personally...she knew 'this was not going to end well.' About an hour later Rachael took me home, and there sitting in my driveway was my silver 2006 Dodge Stratus Limited Edition. Immediately, I turned to Rachael and told her she should leave; I didn't want her to have any part in this. Rachael did leave, but I didn't realize she had also called my mother Bridgette, and told her everything because my cousin was, quite frankly, terrified of what I was going to do.

I entered my house and it was empty, with no Kevin in sight. I cracked open a fresh pint of Seagram's gin and lit my Newport cigarette (my two unwavering, loyal friends), and waited for this bitch to walk in. It was about 9:30 PM before he brought his sorry ass home and I was *good and drunk*, but more importantly, I was ready to "fuck him up." Kevin walked through the door inebriated as hell and just as nonchalantly as he could be like he had not a worry in the world. Without hesitation, I started confronting him about this bitch driving my car. Kevin is steadily denying it. I grab his phone and start scrolling through it. He grabs me and puts me in a bear hug. Instantly, I grab hold of a steak knife and hit his hand. He immediately steps back and looks at his hand. It's smaller than a paper cut and it's not even bleeding. But this bitch looks up and says without blinking, "You stabbed me; I'm calling the cops."

In my head, I'm thinking, *"Are you fucking kidding me??"* This man has been beating my ass since I was about 19 years old, like seriously, 'You had me brainwashed to think it was okay because *it was my fault*—I ran my mouth too much, or I need to stop listening to other people when they tell me about all the shit you were doing. Therefore, he had a right to get mad and put his hands me— *'See what you made me do???'* And on top of all of that, "You have been in and out of jail half of your life, and *I am the only person that has been there for you— even when we weren't together*— I was there! No girlfriend has ever stood by you whenever you were locked up!

I remember when he was in prison, he told me to stop sending him so much money because the officers were starting to look at him like he was dealing drugs. *I was "the one"* who made sure he never wanted for anything—*any* and *every time* he did time—no matter if I was with someone or not.

I'm remembering ALL THESE TIMES of 'Pure Goodness' I gave to this man—years and years of blood, sweat, and tears—being thrown back at me, knocking me down—time after time—weighing down my heart and soul. -- I can no longer breath…no longer get up… And I hear this mother f----- on the phone calling the cops "on Me!" THAT WAS THE FINAL INSULT. As he hangs up the phone, I lunge and jump on his back and commence throwing as many blows as I can—to his torso…anywhere I can reach—which I believe most of them did not connect.

Eventually, he gets a hold of me and grabs my ass and takes me into the bedroom, and throws me fiercely on the bed. We are both wrung out now and breathing hard. Somewhere along the line, he manages to leave the room. By now I am soo tired, I can hardly move. Eventually, I manage to get myself up and, for whatever reason, make my way to the kitchen. With my blithered sight, I see Kevin sitting at the kitchen table—he's drinking my gin now. And like two "True Drunks," who were getting ready to kill each other but show them '*a bottle,*' and they forget what they were doing and lunge for it, I sit down at the table beside him and have a drink and a smoke while waiting for the police to come and 'get *me*.'

The police show up in due time at our door, hear our stories, and based on that immediately inform me that '*I am going to jail,*' so my drunk ass says, pointing to the real culprit, "What about him? He picked me up and threw me on the bed!" which is true. I left out the part it was to stop me from attacking him. I know I was wrong but I had to get him back. *How many assaults on your soul can you take, without striking back??* I cannot believe this shit is really happening. The officers then have a side conversation and decide they don't know exactly what happened so they take us both to jail.-

When we arrive at the jail, I am thoroughly intoxicated by now and Kevin and I are both handcuffed, with one arm each, to a bench. I am pissed that I didn't get a phone call in my mind, not realizing that the police haven't even started the process. Because I am so tiny, I can instantly slip the cuff off my right hand and sashay my little ass right to the officer's door which was closed. I opened it and said with authority, "When am I getting my phone call?? This is some bullshit." Three white police officers were sitting in there and they all turned to look at who the hell was speaking. They looked at me and then at each other like I was crazy—for real—like how and why is this little woman free from her cuffs, and in *our office talking to all 3 of us?* The next thing I knew, the taller one jumped up grabbed me by my shoulder and walked me firmly back down to the bench where Kevin was still cuffed and acting all quiet like some model prisoner. "This time," Mister Policeman tightened that handcuff so tight, that I still had marks on my wrist a week later.

About two hours later, we were both booked into the county jail and I just went to damn sleep. When I woke up, I was given my phone call, so I called my brother Brandon and told him to call my job and let them know I wouldn't be in today. *That* was the most important thing to me—my job, and the last time I was there was yesterday and I had left so abruptly. In no way did I want to jeopardize it. I was thinking and planning, "I will get a bondsman to bail me out." But Brandon did just the opposite; he called my mother and told her I was locked up. Bridgette called my job, and within one hour, my mother bailed me out and was waiting for me outside the jail with her husband Robert. ...Obviously, I was not in the mood for a lecture, but I took what she said *because* it was all true. What stood out the most was when she told me genuinely, "What is it going to take Bella, for you to realize Kevin doesn't give a fuck about you?" That day, my mother Bridgette was dead-on 100% right and that's when I knew my marriage was over. Kevin bailed out too and we went our separate ways. ...And to think...all I wanted was love.

Chapter 9

From *Deep Hell*...I Emerge "A House is not a Home"

Where did I end up after that hellacious nightmare? In the "state of hell," I would say. Following my unforgettable night in the clink, I moved in with my mother and stepfather temporarily. I was one major wreck and had not returned to work. The owner, Dr. Chanigan Vinay, was aware of what was going on and very supportive; that was a huge relief—not having to worry about my job.

At my mother's house, I did nothing but isolate myself in the bedroom and...*drink*—no surprise there. I refused to eat, but finally my stepfather talked me into eating one tuna fish sandwich a day. I complied. This went on for a few weeks. My mom called our primary doctor, Dr. Martin Locksley; he had been our doctor for about 15 years. At some point, I had definitely told him about my alcoholism, so he was well aware of my addiction. He also referred to me as a "functioning alcoholic." I never heard that term before, but I'll gladly take it. It gave a positive perspective to my addiction; my mother would just call me an out-and-out *drunk* when she would get mad at me. I remember Granny taking up for me one day as she chastised my mother, "Bridgette, you're not fooling anyone. You went from heroin to alcohol to prescription pills—just 'cause the doctor prescribes them to you doesn't mean you need to abuse them. You're always in that bedroom high as a kite from that Xanax."-- I loved my Granny and still do. She was my stalwart supporter—the only one I could depend upon.

When my mother called Dr. Locksley, he advised her that I had a nervous breakdown and I should check myself into the psychiatric facility. He was 100 percent correct. I had completely lost it, and honestly, I don't even think it was just Kevin cheating on me that pushed me over the edge. I had refinanced my home for a $25,000 loan for a post-conviction appeal lawyer for Kevin. (God, what I did for that man…) That was a massive weight to carry. My mortgage went from a 6% fixed interest rate at $600 a month to a 9% fixed rate. Now I have a $1,100 a month mortgage; what a dumb fuck I am. The next day I voluntarily signed myself into the Parks Psychiatric Center in New Jersey.

There, I would see Dr. Bruce Thurman, a psychiatrist, on the ward. Dr. Thurman was very pleasant. He used a different tact and tried to hypnotize me, but that shit didn't work (probably because I'm too damn hard-headed). I was supposed to be there for a seven-day evaluation, but after the third day, Dr. Thurman told me he didn't think I had a nervous breakdown. The good doctor diagnosed it as severe depression due to the traumatic separation from my husband; then, he actually complimented me by saying, "I happen to be looking for a medical receptionist. You would have been perfect, but as you are my patient, that would be a conflict of interest." I thanked him for that; it was nice to hear from a physician that a professional person saw my worth. It was Friday, and Dr. Thruman advised me that on Monday he was going to release me. I don't know why I checked myself out, but as soon as the doctor left, I signed the paper releasing myself and went back to my mother's house.

Looking back, all I heard was, 'Everything is good.' When the doctor left, I said, "Uh-uh, I'm leaving. I don't want to be here. He said I was good, and *'I'* because I voluntarily put myself in, I was able to voluntarily leave." *I* signed myself out—I was the one who did it. It was my fault that I left. I wasn't ready, no way, and should have waited through the weekend. Take the excuses away—I guess 'I wanted a bottle' and at that time 'the Gin bottle' was my crutch—couldn't walk, think, or function without it. Nope, you can't take that away from me at this point. This glass bottle and what's in it is all that has comforted me. So, you see, I wasn't in a place to even think about, 'I want to stop drinking.' Let's just say, even though the doctor in his professional opinion may have recommended I leave—*I wasn't ready at that point.* And even though I could hear the faint voice of my Granny sayin,' "It's a 'depressant,' Bella." Duh! Regardless, my brain just needed it.

Kevin and I had now been separated for about two months, and I still had not returned to work since the day I went looking for my vehicle. I was in-and-out of depression. I remember my mother telling me when she called and spoke to Dr. Vinay and told him what was going on; he had responded, "Tell Bella she can take as much time as she needs to get herself together; she will always have her job." I played that tape in my head again and again. It made me very happy that 'my superior, ' a doctor,' would do that for me. I knew that's one thing I had going for me—I was a "great employee." I always have been no matter what job I had. My Granny always told me to be the best you can be at the job, and that's one thing I always did. I know that made her proud.

I remember the day my mother called Dr. Vinay and told him I tried to kill myself; my sweet co-worker Roxie Raines left work and came to the ICU. I didn't know—I was still in a coma—but they all knew and sent me flowers. They showed me so much love and respect. They did, and again, it's a small town, and my mother was going to be honest—why hide it? It's her job; she can't be away forever and not telling this man what's really going on. And he told her, "You know, Bella will always have a job. Tell her to take as much time as she needs." I know I sound like a broken record, but his reaction meant so much to me—maybe it even gave me a reason to live.

When I think about it, Dr. Vinay would have had to shut down one of the offices when I first started—the day the girl got fired and it was 'touch and go' on what to do. However, my response was instant: "Absolutely not! We can rock this out! – Send me one person; we can do three people's jobs! " So, I think it was then he had a lot of respect for me—that I made sure he would be able to continue getting this money from his patients. After all—that's what it's all about—the bottom line is money. Yep, and I was making a lot of money for him at that front desk because 'That's where the buck starts,' where the co-pays and other fees are collected. I have a set response to a patient who tells me, "No, I don't have it." I tell the patient, and always with a smile, "Well, we can reschedule if it's not a sick visit." —Ms. Bella was bringing in to the good doctor $4 to $5,000 just on co-pays and outstanding balances alone weekly. Trust me, the love he had for me—I figured it out—I was bringing in about $120,000 a year, all by myself. That's why Dr. Vinay was giving me raises because I knew the figures, and whenever I told him, "I'm going to need you to bump up my salary because I know what you need—and what I bring in," he did it without question. – He was a businessman.

Dr. Vinay had two other offices, and you can be sure they're not going to ask for money because, quite frankly, "They're scared." I am not scared of anyone. If the patient comes to Roxi Raines and says, "Oh, I have $10 for the co-pay, but I need a pack of cigarettes," she would tell them sweetly, "Oh, just pay it next time." "No, ma'am." --You want the cigarettes, or you want to see the doctor?" That's how I do it. Yeah, I'm tough, but they know I'm fair, and they also know I am 'genuinely' nice. In a small town, people can really see that I care about them. They see that I am a nice, kind person, and when you're like that, people gravitate toward you. Whenever you see me, you see a smile on my face—all the time. It's just a human quality; when you see someone smile, it makes you smile. When I start work, I have a "smile" on my face. Even when I answer the phone, it is with a smile, "This is Bella speaking; how can I help you? " You can hear that smile in your voice, so I try to keep that tone 24-7. Unless somebody comes after me, then well, you get what you get.

The coming week I had a gynecology appointment for my annual pap smear, and the results came back abnormal. Within 48 hours I had an MRI, which showed a tumor the size of a grapefruit—it was lodged right near an artery. I was immediately scheduled for a hysterectomy the very next day. The surgery went well, but honestly, the damn thing devastated me. That was my dream to get married, have children, go to the PTA—that's all I ever wanted. Knowing

I would never have the chance to have a child, I sunk into an even deeper depression...and further into hell.

Given that additional trauma, it's not a big leap that the following week I attempted the ultimate act—"suicide." I gathered up a whole bottle of my blood pressure pills, proceeded to jam every single one of them into my mouth, and to wash them down, what else would I reach for but my forever companion—my bottle of Seagram's gin. I reached for the phone and called Roxi, my co-worker at the clinic who I was close to; I was crying profusely and telling her I no longer wanted to live. --Amazingly, I don't remember any of it.

My mother told me Roxie called her right way. Bridgette was in church at the time, and she left at once. When she got home, she found me passed-out on the kitchen floor. On the way to the hospital, I had three seizures in the ambulance as it raced full speed ahead, sirens screeching. Once there, I was put into a medically induced coma for a week to let my body rest. After that, I was taken to the Neurological Department for another week while they ran tests to make sure I hadn't suffered any brain damage. Luckily, I escaped that blow; no damage had been done. But there was one thing that stuck in my mind. It was something my mother Bridgette said to me, "If you really wanted to kill yourself you wouldn't have told anyone; you would have just done it." That was the day I knew there was no salvaging my mother's and my relationship, *period.*

Following my stay at the hospital, I was immediately sent to the Emory Psychiatric Health Center, as I should have been. I was supposed to be there for 7 days, but after the third day, the psychiatrist Dr. Stoley told me that going through a volatile separation as I had—coupled with having a life-altering surgery—is what pushed me over the edge. Therefore, he deemed me healthy enough to go home. They did attempt to put me on five new medications: one new blood pressure med and four antidepressants. I threw that shit away as soon as I got home. If I wasn't crazy then, I would be after taking all that shit. I continued with my regular blood pressure pills that were prescribed by my primary physician. Amazingly, the following Monday, I went back to work and I was as happy as a clam being back in my element. I was in the bowels of hell but somehow work was always my lifeline.

Kevin and I eventually went to court for the assault charges—which had landed both of us in jail for the night—but because neither one of us wanted to pursue the matter, it was thrown out of court. I then filed for a divorce and had him served at his side chick's apartment (once I was able to obtain her address). On October 12, 2012, my mother and I went to my divorce hearing; Kevin did not show up. I remember the proceedings were almost over and Judge Susan Taylor asked if there was anything I wanted to ask for before she retired to chambers. My mother bent down and whispered in my ear, "Ask for spousal support," and like a dummy I did.

Judge Taylor returned to court about 10 minutes later. She sat down, faced me directly and posed the question, "Do you want to hear the good news or the bad news first?" I answered in a forthright manner, "I prefer the bad news first." Judge Taylor glanced down at her documents and then back at me stating, "I am unable to give you spousal support, because you have taken care of your husband for the entire marriage. - The good news is he is not here, because if he was and asked for spousal support I would have given it to him." Well, ain't that a kick in the butt, but I definitely dodged a bullet that day, and I realized something else—just 'cuz Bridgette is my mother, it doesn't mean she gives out good advice.

By now I was three months behind on my mortgage payments, but since I had a stellar record of 13 years of monthly payments that were 'on time,' they were willing to tack on just three additional months to the end of the loan. But to be frank, I could no longer afford the payments—that and the terrible memories were enough for me to file bankruptcy and forfeit my home. The brutal truth is, "A House is not a Home" if no one's in it—you could be there physically, but if you're really not there, you might as well be ghosts. And my dream? Well, that dream was no longer happening—not now, and not in that house.

-I think I wanted to end my life because not only wasn't my marriage working…but in my eyes—how am I gonna rebuild my credit; how am I going to keep a mortgage going, at $1,000 a month, and *my Grandmother* would be turning over in her grave to know that I have destroyed something that none of the others were able to do on their own—without their husbands—get a home built! And not just any home but a brand-new home that was built from 'the ground up,'—I truly started from "ground zero," baby. All the others—they bought homes that were already built. To do that on your own and then I lost it?? That's what broke me. It was the damn man Kevin, "You lied to me. I did all this for you and you come home and do the same shit you said you didn't want to do anymore." It broke my heart and my ass and my hard-earned pocketbook I'd worked for all my life. --"It was the gross disrespect and the point that I know my Granny was turning over in her grave. It probably wasn't even the marriage itself. It was, "How dare you allow me to spend 25 grand on your ass, and you come home and do the 'same shit'?" "Not today, sir. NO. -- Yea they do—really try to break you—get you for everything your worth."

So, I moved myself to a one-bedroom waterfront condo on beautiful South Orange Bay, New Jersey. My thinking was if I am going to take a loss on the house, I might as well live better than I was for the same $1,000 payment. Granted, I am paying someone else's mortgage off, but I was starting all over—*with no credit*—so fuck it.

It is now 2013. I was an expert at my job, I'm back livin,' workin,' and doin,'and also had time to cruise the internet on BlackPeopleMeet.com in between checking in patients. Scrolling through the site, I noticed a man named Chike Diamini. He certainly wasn't a looker—ya think I'd have my fill of that—but this man appeared so nice and kind. He was from Nigeria just like my Uncle Michael, so that was a good thing. My Uncle Michael was the greatest and best man I had ever met.

I sent this gentleman Chike a message and he responded back immediately. Things are looking up… We continued to chat on the website and about a week later, we upgraded to text and phone calls. It was refreshing to talk with someone who was highly intelligent and had the degrees to match. After about two months, we met at a Nigerian restaurant on the South Orange Bay which was a central meeting point—about 45 minutes away from each of us. It was an enjoyable dinner; I had oxtails and plantains—you remember how much I enjoyed the oxtails my Uncle Michael made! My date Chike had Joll of rice and Egusi soup, traditional Nigerian dishes. The conversation flowed between us like we had known each other for years. Chike had been in New Jersey for six months on a work visa; he was working for his Uncle Kabila Diamini who had his own computer marketing business. Chike and I continued to date for a few months, and then he moved in with me. Things seemed to be taking their natural course.

Chike Diamini had been living with me for about 6 months and continuing his hour and half commute to his Uncle Kabili's business. On May 15th, we decided to get married at the courthouse. Was it too fast? I don't know, never crossed my mind, just going with the flow. Within four months Chike said the commute of an hour and a half was just too far a drive so he decided to switch jobs and was hired at the Whole Foods Market. I was okay with it, but I did ask him, "Are you a manager there?" Chike replied without hesitation, "No, I am a stocker." I replied instantly perturbed, "Why the fuck are you a stocker when you have 15 degrees?? - I am confused." Chike came up with some bullshit excuse about his visa—how he needed to get new paperwork processed to work in his field of Computer Software Development. He explained, "It's' a *long* process that will take about a year." I realized then I had just been *played.*

My dilemma was this. Do I put his ass out and divorce him? Or do I keep him in the house so I am not alone? Because, you see, by now my drinking has gone from a one-gallon bottle of Seagram's gin a week—straight no chaser—to "two" gallon bottles a week. In my head I'm thinking, I needed someone in the house in case I drank myself to death; at least, he can notify my family and job. I was a "functioning alcoholic" and had been one for the past fifteen years. But now, I drank every day, from the moment I came home from work—for about two hours—then I would eat and go to sleep. The next morning, I would get up, go to work, come home and do the same shit every day, like clockwork. I decided to keep Chike there but moved his bitch ass out of my bed and on to the couch. Fuck you.

One day I was lying in bed watching TV, and I turned on YouTube, and I ran across a YouTuber by the name of "Funky Dineva." I was enamored. This man was so funny, articulate, and most of all he was telling *his truth* no matter who likes it or not. As he would say, "No matter—good, bad, or indifferent." I was hooked and every day when I came home from work, I couldn't wait to see what he had posted next. I knew I would be a fan for life. "Funky Dineva" was a good thing that came into my life. Thank you, Funky.

In 2016, the University of New Jersey Hospital in New Jersey was hiring Front Desk Coordinators for a new office they were opening; it was about twenty minutes away from me. They were starting out the new hires making more money than I was, and I had more experience than they did. I applied immediately and following my interview was hired two weeks later. Now I had to notify Dr. Vinay and put in my two weeks' notice. I knew in advance he was going to be pissed, but when I relocated four years ago, I was driving a two-hour daily commute (to and from). It was a no brainer; I was leaving regardless.

After receiving my two weeks' notice, Dr. Vinay called me into his office. He started by offering me a raise, but when I told him it wasn't about the money—that I was just tired of the commute—just as I predicted, he got very pissed, because let's be honest, most rich people *think* and *know* money can buy pretty much anybody. There were quite a few curse words thrown back and forth. Basically, I *did not leave* with his blessings, but years later we will make amends when I am diagnosed with having a heart attack in my sleep in 2020. I emailed Dr. Vinay my Stress test results so that he could confirm that I am good-to-go. Dr. Vinay concurred and also told me that he and I will always have a special bond.

April 15, 2016, was my first day of work at the University of New Jersey Hospital, in New Jersey. I was so happy. I would be working for two doctors: Dr. Christopher Anderson was a nice-looking man, very tall, and had a beautiful tan. He stood about 6'3" and weighed 200 lbs. He had bright hazel eyes with dark brown hair which he wore in a buzz cut. Then there was Dr. Myra Johnson, the first African American female doctor I have ever worked for. She was absolutely stunning. She stood 5'7" and weighed about 170 lbs. She had radiant caramel skin with greenish-gray eyes, and she wore her hair in a platinum blonde, short, tapered cut. I flourished as usual, and about two years later, a new doctor was hired for the practice, Dr. Brian Chester, a cardiologist.

The only problem was there was no room for Dr. Chester in that office, so someone needed to be moved to a new office as his Front Office Coordinator/Medical Assistant. I was chosen by default. I was the only Coordinator there that had experience and could perform a dual role position. I was never officially trained for Medical Assistance, but I was what you call 'grandfathered-in.' I had hands-on-training from the doctors versus actually attending school and learning via books, tests and exams.

On June 20th,2018 I started my first day with Dr. Brian Chester at the University of New Jersey Hospital New Jersey, Pulmonology Office. Dr Chester did not look like the doctors I was used to working for. He was very overweight, short in stature, and had unsightly coffee stains on his shirt which was so wrinkled, it looked as if he had just retrieved it from a dirty clothes hamper and threw it on. What the fuck have I gotten myself into now?

Don't get me wrong Dr. Chester was one of the most intelligent doctors I have ever worked for, but he had a horrible bedside manner! He would come to work late and have patients waiting for hours. He would argue with patients; it was awful. I felt like a referee because I never knew if he was going to insult or argue with his patients. I would have to be the intermediary and go into the room and calm things down. But on the flipside, he was so, so kind to me, and he taught me more things in the few months I worked for him than I ever learned in the eleven years working for Dr. Vinay. The man knew his shit. I was reading/interpreting EKG's and stress tests like an expert. I love to learn so I was thoroughly enjoying working for him—outside of him being rude as fuck to his patients.

So, at this time in my life, I am working for a combative doctor, and I go home to a scammer. My life is not a 'bed of roses'—not one in sight—more accurately, a 'bed of thorns.' I arrive home, take my shower, grab my gin bottle, light up a Newport, and turn on Funky Dineva. I am watching his My Hair is Layed Like *Real Housewives of Atlanta* series, and I am being thoroughly entertained. He is not only informative, but he cracks me the hell up. It's sad when the only happiness you have in your life is from your TV, but it is what it is.

On November 21, 2018, Chike received a call from his mother saying his oldest son had fallen out of a tree and broke his arm in two places. Chike flew back to Nigeria two days later, with his return flight scheduled for December 23rd. A few days later, I went to my mother's house inebriated as hell for Thanksgiving dinner. My Aunt Joan, my brother Brandon, my stepfather Robert and my mother who was high on Xanax were all there. We were all eating the holiday dishes and enjoying our conversation, when the phone rang. My mother answered it and all of a sudden her smile disappeared and her voice changed; she sounded like she was about to cry. When she hung up, my Aunt Joan spoke first, "Bridgette what's wrong?" My mother was holding back tears, blurting out that our cousin Charlotte called because her twin brother Charles was talking about killing himself. – I snapped—my response was *immediate and fierce.* Charles was my teenage cousin who had molested me when I was a little girl. *This bitch* is crying over him??? At once, I started screaming, "Are you fucking <u>kidding me</u>?? -- You are crying over the *mutherfucker* that molested me???" Bridgette immediately screams back at me, "Well you changed your story!" That was a fucking lie! I had never changed my story. - There was nothing to change! I am up on my feet to confront her, "*You are a fucking liar* and <u>I hate you.</u>"

I leave the house at once, with force and thunder in my wake. My Aunt Joan runs after me calling out, "Bella, I am so sorry; I didn't know!" I answered her abruptly, "Of course you didn't! Granny and

Bridgette told me to pretend it didn't happen." Joan then tempered her voice, "Bella, just go to 'my house.' You're drunk; it's too far for you to drive home." I drive home anyway and am replaying this shit in my head…why would she protect him again?? My Aunt Joan called me to make sure I made it home safely, and she added, "I confronted Bridgette and she admitted it." I said, "Fuck Bridgette," and hung up. -- I was OVER it.

On December 20th I received a call from the office manager Mark Robinson. He was giving me a heads-up that Dr. Chester has a meeting today with the higher ups regarding his 6-month follow up evaluation…and it is not going to be pretty. I knew he had a meeting because Dr. Chester had been freaking out all week about it and I knew it was going to be bad. Just last week a patient of his was so upset when she left, she told me she was reporting him. So, I was aware in advance what was in store for him. What I didn't know was how it would affect me. About 4:00 PM, I received the call from Mark letting me know Dr. Chester was fired on the spot. The higher ups felt he was a liability, which he was. And I asked, "What happens to me?" Mark answered, "We don't have any space at your old office, but there is another office in Newark, NJ. You will go to that one." I felt hopeless and depressed; now, I have to start all over with another doctor in a new office. I was just waiting for Chike my husband/my roommate to return. At least I wouldn't be in the condo alone.

December 23rd comes and I finally get a call from Chike. He says something about his sons wanting him to say a few days more, so he is changing his return flight to January 3rd. I'm cool with it. However, on the work front, the office manager hasn't found a doctor for me to work for, so I am just packing up our office things on a daily basis. I start feeling my mood turn into an oppressive, abysmal state and decide to call Dr. Martin Locksley (my Primary physician) and let him know I needed a break from working. (*Frankly,* I just needed to drink my gin.)

Dr. Locksley agreed with my request, "I will put you on leave from work for two weeks, and then you follow up with me at my office, and we will decide your next step which are two options at this point: continue to drink and get a disability check or the "R" word. Yes folks, the Doc felt I was that far gone that I would qualify for disability or I can go to Rehab. I took the deal and drank non-stop for the next two weeks all alone. Now, I am chucking a gallon straight every two days. I am falling asleep on the floor in the hallway. I can't remember if I ate—I would look in the kitchen sink to see if I had dirty dishes. That's how I knew if I had eaten the day before. It was bad, *real bad.* I knew I was no longer functioning, *period.*

On January 2, 2019, Chike called the night before he was to return—to let me know he wasn't coming back "ever." Honestly, I had an inkling when he postponed it the first time, that it was a distinct possibility he is a "ghost in the wind." I was still pissed, upset and humiliated, but I got over it quickly, because amazingly my hard head finally realized and knew the only thing I needed in my life at this time was—*"Rehab."* I already knew what I was going to do on my follow-up visit with Dr. Locksley. "I am going to a Drug and Alcohol Rehabilitation Center." It's the only choice I have—*or I will die.* For days, for months, for years this is the moment you've been hoping for, working toward against all odds, and when that single moment of revelation occurs, it comes so naturally, you can't believe all the m----f---- steps, the shit you had to wade through, the jagged rocks you had to climb just to get to the "first marker," I DO NOT WANT TO DIE, and the arrow direction says "REHAB," and you are finally ready to turn in that direction.

Some part of your mind has clicked in and you acknowledge your life is at stake here—and 'I will die a lot quicker if I go on disability.' Going to work every day is the only thing that has saved me so far from drinking all day--24 hours straight...minus unconscious sleep. "Shout out to Funky Dineva again!" Like he says, *"I went to work and called the Employee Assistant Program line and told them, people, I have a drinking problem and 'I need help.'"* It was the best decision I had ever made in my entire life. Thank you, Bella. We just took the 1st step outa hell!

Chapter 10

"Revelation – Rehab" Deep Hell to SHELTER

On January 8, 2019, I took the first step out of hell and chose *To Live!* Finally, I *took the step* that would "Save my Life." Courageously, I took a pen in hand and signed myself into the New Jersey Recovery Center for their thirty-day program to rehabilitate from drugs or alcoholism. Mine of course was the latter and IT SAVED MY LIFE. The entire time I was in the Rehab Center, I did not call a single person, nor did I tell anyone in my family where the fuck I was. During this period, I have absolutely *no one* and am *totally on my own.* - I am just fine with this.

The first thing I did was request authorization from the management to have access to my cell phone so I could pay my monthly bills. In rehabilitation centers, you are prohibited from having access to your cellphones due to safety reasons, as anyone could have their supplier (yes, as in "drugs") come to the center to provide them with drugs or whatever else they are addicted to. The cellphone would be a direct pipeline to the outside world, and therefore it is forbidden. That's what made my request so strange and unusual.

A week after I had made it, I was escorted into the office of the manager of the rehab center, Mrs. Katherine McAdams. Interestingly, she was very polite and apologized for the delay in getting back to me. Her eyes raised quietly to mine—with no hint of judgement or attitude—and she notified me they had never had that kind of request before. She stated that the usual state of affairs is that once the clients end up here, they are broke and destitute. Fortunately for me, I was continuing to be paid bimonthly from my employer, the University of the New Jersey Hospital, where I worked before I took leave. Given these circumstances, I sat in her office for about 30 minutes, while she attentively watched me click on the various apps on my phone that were connected to my bank account to pay my bills. This truly was a first for the manager of a rehab center to witness, and I could tell she was duly impressed.

After I was finished with my bill payments, I thanked Mrs. McAdams, and as I was walking out of her office, her voice stopped me, and she said, "Again, this is the first time we've had this situation, and I just want to say I am very impressed to see how financially responsible you are." That really made me feel good. Again, a professional person was seeing "my worth" despite circumstances that have landed me at the bottom of my gut and soul.

While in rehab, I *thrived* in these surroundings. I loved it! I had my first African American therapist, Ebony. She was drop-dead gorgeous, with beautiful chocolate skin and a bright white smile that would light up a room. She wore her natural black hair in beautiful box braids. She even advised me of a therapy that was especially beneficial to me. It was called 'shock trauma,' and it allowed the possibility of me being able to sleep on my back again—which would be a Godsend. If you remember, ever since I was a little girl and molested by my cousin, I have not been able to 'physically' sleep on my back. The explanation I got from previous therapists was that my mind is still processing this *traumatic childhood event.* Every time I try to sleep on my back, a bad trigger is activated, and mentally, I feel like I will be touched down there again because that is the position in which I was violated. It has become my most vulnerable area and the one I protect the most by sleeping on my stomach or side—ever since the night I lost my innocence.

In these very different but for the most part positive surroundings, I also met a beautiful stud named Deanna from Virginia; she was there for alcoholism too. They called her Dee; she was smitten with me. (I know what you're thinking; no, you are not there for that.) But yes, within two weeks of us talking, we smashed and I decided A MAJOR DECISION IN MY LIFE—*I am no longer playing these games with these men. "I am over being bisexual."* Who would have thought I am coming out of rehab both 'sober as a judge,' and a 'whole lesbian'? In this place, I experienced Enlightenment and Transformation of both body and spirit!

Because I had excellent insurance, I was able to extend my rehabilitation to a 90-day program facility located in Atlanta, Georgia, which I definitely needed to do. Thirty days would not have been long enough for me, and statistics confirm that those who have chosen only a 30-day treatment program have an 85% relapse rate in the 1st year. So, after my thirty days were up at the Recovery Center of NJ, I had two weeks before I would report to the Atlanta facility. My lease was up on the condo the following month, so I decided to notify my landlord that I was relocating out of state, and the nice people allowed me to vacate my lease a month early without penalizing me. I was very happy and relieved about this because, frankly, I didn't know where I was going after rehab; the only thing *I did know* was, 'I'm *not* going back to New Jersey.' I knew living in New Jersey was no longer an option. Hazard signs abound there; I would *immediately* relapse if I went back there. At this point, I'm thinking I would either relocate to Pennsylvania or Florida.

However, I had two weeks to kill before I had to check-in at the new Rehab Center in Georgia—so I decided to go and visit my father in Tallahassee, Florida—a state very near Georgia. He was happy to see me, and at the time, my dad was in a *"normal drinking"* mode...nothin' heavy...unlike his visit to my house—*where we both drank like "fishes,"* or the first time he came to New Jersey to tell us about my 'other half-sister,' Yvette, who was literally dying from alcoholism, and yet we 'all' drank incessantly. For God's sakes, what does it take? A sobering question I'm answering as I get ready for the

BIG ONE---"THE 90-DAY REHAB PROGRAM," in Atlanta, Georgia.

So, in the beginning of March 2019—after my visit to see my father—I headed to the Ambrosia Treatment Center in Atlanta, GA. There, I would continue to flourish and grow, even more so with the counselling of another African American therapist by the name of Simone. She was short and a little on the heavy side, standing at 5 feet and weighing about 200 lbs. She had creamy almond skin with hazel eyes and wore her hair in a short pixie cut which was fire engine red to compliment her skin...which it definitely did. She was utterly amazing and such an important person in my healing process. I completed my therapy at the end of June and it helped to shine a penetrating light on the demons living inside and outside that caused me to drink in the first place. The professional treatment Simone offered provided me with concrete coping mechanisms which I never had before on the outside.

This time when I walked out into the open air after 90 days, I felt more "whole and intact." My body, my mind, my spirit had all been flailing around like a lost tornado and in deep pain from the beatings I'd sustained for so many years. As I've said before, the mental and emotional beatings were far worse than the physical ones. Rehab had provided a respite away from everything and everybody, a place where I could concentrate "just on me," and the professional people I encountered knew their shit, my shit, and could help me deal with it. Nothing is perfect but when I left, I was a better person for it and decided to embark upon 'new beginnings' and relocate to an entirely different city. I checked in to an extended-stay-hotel for about two weeks; there I could spend time figuring out my next move.

There were two more weeks remaining before I was to return to work in New Jersey. I made the decision to stay in Pittsburgh and rent a one-bedroom apartment for $1100 a month. For my work information on the application, I used the University of New Jersey since I was still technically employed there. Then, I put in my two-weeks' to the University a day later. Now, I was just 'looking for a job,' and not so stressed about going back to one. *Stress, over-stress, abundant stress over long periods of time are what caused my "fall to hell" in the first place. This time,* I made sure I had a cushion and had saved up a few thousand dollars; add to that a few credit cards—one with a $10,000 thousand dollar limit—and I had some breathing space. Rehab gave me time to think and regain my sustenance on many levels. That's why today I was standing on my own two feet and not in a state of panic.

However, fast forward a few more months into 2020, and I was still unemployed even though I was going on at least two interviews a day and still…nothing. Six months later, on December 14, 2020, my luck changed and I was hired by Fed-Ex as a customer service representative. Boy did it feel good to be working again! I am the *model* for "The Working Girl." I marched myself into the office for work—all excited and upbeat—and worked straight through…until March of 2020 when we were sent home from work due to Covid. Well, initially I looked at it as 'positive.' I was always a "homebody," so I could adapt to working at home. This was perfect.

Out of the blue, I received a call from my roommate/husband Chike. He called and asked why I never reached out or responded to his messages; I let him know I had been in rehab. Then he asked a strange question, "Did I still want to stay married?" I snapped back, *"Hell no!* - Why would I?" Given that, he then asked me, "Did I want to file for the divorce?" Again, I responded abruptly, *"Hell no! - You file,* don't you think you got enough out of me?? *Damn you,* you got your green card off me! Can't you spend *'your own damn money'* and file??' Freakin' men! Chike was in Detroit, Michigan when he filed. Our divorce was final a few months later. I told Chike to send me a certified copy so I could have my name legally changed back to my maiden name. *Life is getting better and better!* Honestly, that was a real fear I had; if I couldn't locate the man, how would I file for divorce?

Life is moving merrily along and in April of 2022 I went on a lesbian dating site called Taimi. I started chatting with a retired deputy sheriff by the name of Desiree Beckford. Desiree was working part time as a security guard at Walmart and she had one daughter who was 24. Desiree was about 5'5," nice brown skin and weighed about 140 pounds; she was a small lady. We chatted online for a while and then upgraded to text and phone calls. I thoroughly enjoyed talking to this intelligent woman. I hate to say it but I see things so differently as a lesbian. I cannot tolerate *"ghetto, mean, hood-rat behavior. Period."* period. I don't care how beautiful these women are, I just can't do it. Please believe me, *I know* I am not the most intelligent woman out there, but please do me the favor of *'knowing how to speak proper English before approaching me.'* Anyway, we went out on a few dates; and it was very nice, but we still haven't had sex yet. I still wasn't sure how far I wanted to take this. Trust me I know "I am broken"...*but healing*. You have to take it very slowly, and very carefully. A few months later, I felt more confident and I decided to give Desiree some action. It was cool, nothing spectacular.

Our family reunion was coming up; it was taking place during the fourth of July weekend. In the past, we've had great times as a family during the 4th of July holidays, so I decided to go home to New Jersey. I told Desiree I would leave Saturday morning, about 7:00 AM, and return home Sunday night. Right off the bat, she seemed like she had a problem with it, but I didn't care, I was going regardless. I got there and completely surprised my family. No one knew I was coming (just like no one knew I was going into rehab.) Let me tell you, I had a ball! I remember I had left my purse in my mother's trunk because I didn't have pockets in my pants, and I didn't want to walk around carrying a phone in my hand all day. And to be perfectly honest, some members of the family are crackheads—and will steal anything for their habit—so, I didn't want to leave my purse unattended...in case there were some thieves running amuck.

However, about two hours later, I went to the car to get my phone and check my messages. *This fool Desiree* had called me "thirty-seven times" and left "twenty-four voicemails." Count them! I immediately called her and she went *berserk,* "Why are you not answering your phone? Who are you down there fucking?" I was flabbergasted at her behavior and shot back, "Are you fucking kidding me?? I am at a fucking family reunion! - If you call me one more time I will block your ass," then I hung up on her, furious. The damn woman keeps at it and calls me again! This time, I immediately blocked her.

Truthfully, I had a blast that night no crazies are going to block my fun. I went out with my cousins to the Club in the next town and danced *all night long*. …And get this…I even ran into my ex-husband Kevin and his new wife. Ha! Kevin looked like he'd seen a ghost but he managed to smile as brightly as he could. I have to say, 'it was nice to see him too;' it had been 11 years since we divorced. I turned to his new wife with a genuine smile on my face, and introduced myself, "Hi, I am Bella, Kevin's first wife. Nice to meet you," and then I sashayed *my fine ass* back to the dance floor *killing it*… at least, in my mind. Ha! I was quite proud of myself—how I handled that after that man had ripped my heart out. Yea, it was water under the bridge, but more importantly *I* had grown. – My life didn't *'depend on,' 'rely on 'a man.'* I was standing on my own two feet…just fine. That night, I stayed at my cousin's house and the next morning, I drove back to Pennsylvania.

Once I was home and settled in, I decided to unblock Desiree and have an adult conversation—so I thought. Desiree was still screaming like a maniac on the phone, so…I just hung up. She continued to call for a little bit and I let my voicemail pick up, and then she stopped calling. Something told me to check my voicemail. I had a feeling something was wrong. I checked my voicemail. *Desiree was on her way over to my apartment to blow her brains out with her 38 revolver that she kept in her glove compartment*—which I knew for a fact was there—because I saw it in her car the last time if we could go out to dinner. Immediately, I called her back but she didn't answer. I continued to call, and finally she picked up. Sincerely concerned, I asked her if she was ok, and she answered with, "I'm on the way over to your house to blow my brains out." She wanted me to watch. OMG. At once, I called the police and told them what was going on.

The police arrived before she did and I went outside and spoke to them. They waited for about an hour but Desiree never showed up. I called her back to check in on her, but she still wasn't answering. The police decided to keep a squad car outside my apartment until the next day in case she showed up. A few hours later, Desiree called me from her home crying up a storm; she had never left. I tried to talk to her and be of solace but she was so depressed she wasn't listening to me. I told her gently, "Go to sleep and call me in the morning when you wake up and we will talk about it."

The next morning around 9 o'clock, Desiree called. She sounded much more emotionally stable. We talked for a few hours. I was able to explain to her that she was still going through the trauma from her ex-fiancé who had left her earlier in the year. As for me, I explained to her in a rational voice, 'It cannot possibly be about me because you haven't known me long enough to be that emotionally attached.' I shared with her my own trauma that I have been going through and told her that she really needs to start therapy. Desiree agreed and scheduled a consultation appointment for two weeks later. She continued to call periodically, but I explained to her very clearly that we were done, but I am here to support her as a friend. That is why I would not cut off all communication with her until I knew she was in therapy and getting the help she needed.

Desiree called two weeks later to tell me about her therapy consultation; she let me know she was in a much better head space, and then asked if we could go out to dinner. I told her to quit playing with me; I am not doing this today, and I told her to keep up the therapy, that it works. After that, I blocked Desiree, and never unblocked her. – I was strong enough and 'wise enough' to set my own boundaries. Through my own therapy, I knew now how important this was to be able to set your own boundaries. I wished Desiree well in my heart, but from this moment forward, I, 'Bella,' came first in my life now. My responsibility was to *me*.

...And I would need all my wits about me as on December 8, 2022, a massive challenge reared its head. FedEx notified us they were closing the office permanently, and our last day would be March 10th. Are you kidding?? Panic started to set in at once, and before I knew it was March 10th. This time I had no new job prospects in sight. My lease was up in April and I was living paycheck to paycheck—just like a lot of Americans were—and post-Covid sure added to the fray. All my credit cards were maxed out, and I had nowhere to go, nor anyone to call for help. In a world of more than a billion people in it...I have absolutely no fucking body to call for help. --It was a profoundly sad feeling which I have never felt before.

On April 1, 2023, I hit absolute *"rock bottom"*—the basement of hell's abyss. Throw away your keys, Bella. You don't have control of or in need of any keys where you're going... You are about to enter another world. - I left my apartment behind and entered the Samantha B. Brown Shelter in Pittsburgh, PA, the only shelter in the state that allowed convicted sex offenders (both men and women) to reside within their walls. As I walked through these strange doors for the first time, I knew only one thing—no matter if I am in the White House, a penthouse, or this shelter, I will always be myself. -- Bella is Bella...no matter where I go.

Chapter 11

"Rising from The Abyss ~ Through the Open Door"

I used to say I can adapt to any environment, but now I realize that any environment I am in adapts to me. From the moment I rolled up to that facility, arriving in a nice-looking car, dressed in nice clothes—the way I always dress, carrying myself with respect—with a nice-looking piece of luggage trailing behind me, every eye I encountered was on me. Not because I thought I was some prima donna, but because that's who I am. I don't change for anyone or any place. I didn't think I was more or less than anyone else. In fact, I was just like them—I hit "rock bottom," just like each of them did. The only difference was I didn't look like them.

My journey here came from a higher path traveled—at the age of 25 years old, I had built and owned my own home. Having the good fortune of being raised by a strong woman pillar like my Granny, I had a different set of values lifting me up. And though the street environment was all around me, I strived not to let it overtake me—end up on the streets as a drug addict that needed to fuel my habit. However, I did become an alcoholic, albeit a "functioning alcoholic"—so at least I was able to work on a daily base and strive toward my dreams.

That's the other factor that differentiated me from my Shelter mates—sadly, many had no dreams. I would find their lives were based on sheer survival—how and where to live or die every day of the week—dreams were non-existent. Where and how they were born, not having a tower of strength and wisdom like our Granny—a formidable woman who could not be knocked down and built a foundation for her family—it was our matriarch who instilled in us the possibility of dreams. She herself became the prime example; coming from the humblest of beginnings, our grandmother set out with courage and unrelenting stamina to pioneer a trail of hope for her family. She not only *talked about* what was possible but she became the enduring Model. She held the torch for us creating indomitable "Women," who could fall to the depths of hell and somehow still see a light and find the wherewithal to crawl to it.

Yes, what I have in common with these women Shelter-mates is—we ALL fell to the bottom of the barrel, whether you were already scraping the basement floor and fell even further to the abyss, or you who climbed your way up to a 'higher' mountain and fell from a higher place. There is a caveat—the higher you rise, the deeper the fall. But it is *these Women,* who looked at me like I was a 'duck out of water,' who would teach *"me"* great lessons of life that I had yet to learn. It was these Women who would ultimately help me realize the *real meaning* of HOME.

Day one in this new world was in many ways the 1st day of my life. Departing from my Uber with matching suitcase and duffel bag, I rang the bell on the side of the building and noticed the few benches that were outside were populated with men and women...all staring at me. I smiled genuinely at all of them, and then turned my head back and focused on the lady that was screaming through the microphone. Then the door opened and I entered into my *new home,* The Samantha B. Brown Shelter, approached the desk and advised the receptionist at the window, whose name was Ms. Bernice Jackson, that I, Bella St. Patrick, was *'in the house,'* so to speak. She then had me sit at a desk and fill out a packet of papers. The packet consisted primarily of the rules and regulations of the shelter.

After I completed the paperwork, I was escorted down a hallway to my new living quarters which was basically a refurbished gym with 50 cots—46 of them occupied with women of all ages and walks of life. With a cursory glance I say to myself, "This is jail to me… without a paycheck; fuck it, it is what it is." I then unpacked some of my belongings and put them into my chest located at the foot of my cot and locked it away. This constitutes your living space; a cot and each one has a footlocker of sorts at the end of your bed. Then I walked back into the dayroom where approximately 20 women were watching TV and playing cards. I decided to sit down and just observe.

After about an hour, I began to feel a little hungry so I walked up to Ms. Jackson's desk and asked politely what time dinner is served, and may I see the menu to see what we're having. Ms. Jackson looked up at me like I had two heads, pushed her glasses down to see me better, and started shrieking, "What do you mean *'menu'?* - You will eat what they feed you; dinner is at 5:00 PM." I answered, "Ok, thank you Ma'am," managing my nicest tone, while chastising myself in my head, "What were you thinking you idiot?? This is a shelter, not a fancy restaurant!"

I heard someone from the other side of the dayroom comment loudly so that she could be heard throughout, "Well, we know she don't eat out of a trash can." There were a few looks and talkbacks in response, but I immediately told myself, "Don't you look over there, because I know if I see whoever said that I would automatically picture her *eating a cheeseburger standing inside of a dumpster*—every time she spoke to me." What is wrong with me?? I sat back down, and suddenly a few of the ladies sauntered over and started giving me compliments: "Wow you are beautiful! Your outfit is cute," and then they start asking me a million questions. "What are *you* doing here? You look like you don't belong here. What happened? Do you have kids? Where are you from?" I answer a few of the questions, and then I hear them call for Dinner Time. Actually, I was kinda glad for the distraction.

I start walking with the ladies to the cafeteria (in my mind…I got this…I will be okay). However, entering the cafeteria, it happens—this is when I break down. I'm casually walking in line with everyone else and when I get to the front where the volunteers are dishing out the food, I immediately say hello brightly. "How is everyone's evening?" That's just me; I am a very friendly, outgoing person and I always try to keep a smile on my face (at work, at The Shelter, on the phone, at The White House, or in the middle of a riot). Suddenly, the volunteers glance up at me and stop what they're doing. It was four older Caucasian women, one Caucasian man, and two African American women and their eyes all are turned directly toward me. You can see the confusion on their faces—'wait does she work here??' She can't possibly be one of the residents.' *But I was.* -- I thanked them graciously for my food and went to sit down while I watched all the people in the cafeteria—men and women gawking at me, 'the new resident.'

As I started eating my meal, which consisted of a tuna casserole, green beans, and peaches, I could feel a tear forming in my eye. *Where was I? – What am I doing here? I'm just trying to be friendly and nice under very challenging circumstances and in a strange environment—I have just arrived at the 'bottom of hell,' and trying to make the most and best of it.* I was feeling some kind of way I never felt before. Instantly, I reached for my phone and called my brother Brandon and asked him one question: "How in the hell did I go from volunteering to *'feed the homeless'* last year to now *'being homeless?'* My brother answered in the best words he could think of, "Life. - Shit happens." I hung up with Brandon, finished my food, and went back to the day room.

After an hour of watching TV there, I found a section with a small bookshelf filled with about 25 books. I was so happy it was there and immediately grabbed a book I saw by Lee Child called, *The Enemy*; I love the Jack Reacher novels. I decided to go back into the living quarters to continue putting my things away and as I sat on my cot, I heard some arguing about two rows over. I could tell it was between an African American and a Caucasian woman going at it. They're screaming back and forth like banshees…and then I hear the African American woman shout out, "You racist bitch!" and the Caucasian woman instantly shoots back with attitude, "Nigga, I ain't racist!" I'm like 'oh shit,' and then I hear the security guards hurrying over and they break them apart. I took out my night clothes and went and showered.

After finishing, I sat on my cot and started reading my book. I was in my element. The fiasco continued off and on, and at one point I couldn't comprehend what I was reading. So, I turned on my trusty Funky Dineva at 8 PM on YouTube, put on my headphones and as usual, enjoyed the hell out of his commentary. It always makes me feel better about the situation I am in…like this one…pretty radical circumstances wouldn't you say? Though lookin' at me with my headphones on—concentrated and contented—I felt like I was in the "eye of the storm," the only place that was calm and peaceful when all hell's breaking loose around you.

Every time I go outside at least 30 of the men black and white all speak to me daily, grinning. It's okay I grin and speak back. A few days later I made a public service announcement in the cafeteria, "Hey I am a "whole" lesbian and I am not interested in no one here, period!- So, it was not a rumor; you heard it straight from the horse's mouth." I didn't have too many problems with anyone crossing the line after that, other than the occasional asshole comment, but I was fine with that. I'm a grown ass woman, little as hell, but *still,* I'm a grown ass woman!

After about two weeks I had my first visit with my social worker, Ms. Monica Spencer, a petite African American woman; I'm guessing in her early thirties. Ms. Spencer was very pleasant and she explained the process of applying for a Housing Voucher. She gave me the proper forms to take with me and fill out, and related other information I would also need, such as my Birth Certificate, Social Security card, and Checking and Savings Account info. Ms. Spencer advised me the entire process from start to finish usually takes about six to eight months, and it is best if *I am unemployed,* because I will get more money for my voucher. I thanked her and left the office. I was already walking downtown daily (which was about two miles one way) applying for jobs. Ms. Spencer had me fucked up; I am not built to sit around doing nothing all day…*best to be unemployed?? That's definitely f---ed up!* ...Besides, in The Shelter, who gets 'a voucher' is determined by 'who needs it the worst,' so of course that means the mentally ill, the sickly, the women with the kids come first, and then you have the single people like me, which by their program, I would have been there forever sittin' on my ass waitin' for a voucher.

It's May and by now it's like *Cheers*, the TV show, where 'everyone knows my name.' I am not going to lie. I kind of made shelter life fun; who would have thought it? I pretty much get along with everyone; the ladies are between the ages of 18 and 77.

I must think I was a Tamron Hall on *Dateline* because I was always interviewing every single woman on the details of their personal story—wondering how they ended up here in The Shelter—and wow, the stories they told. I have always lived by the saying "There is always somebody out there worse off than you." How true that is, *especially 'here.'* Here, you can't feel too sorry for yourself because some of the women's stories are *far worse* than your own...and you've gone through some pretty *deep shit* yourself, but 'here,' you are humbled. They don't have a mean bone in their bodies, until you do something to them. I believe we're here for a purpose. – I have hit rock-bottom. There's a reason why I'm here. I have to figure out 'why.'

Let me play my Tamron Hall role for a few moments and introduce you to the unique, one-of-a-kind women who are my Shelter mates:

- Connie Bradford is a 74-year-old single, Caucasian woman with no kids. Everyone calls her "granny." You could tell she was in her 70's by the many wrinkles that covered her frail face. Of course, I was raised well, so I didn't want to disrespect anyone, especially the ones who were raised by wolves, so I would never mention that any woman looked 'old.' Connie's big thing is she loves to date younger men—hey, no one's judging here. She was always lending them money or taking care of them. The last man she dated was 37-years-old, and he scammed her out of four thousand dollars, fleeced her out of everything she had. Thanks to that young idiot, "granny" lost her apartment and that's how she ended up in The Shelter. Scamsters come in all sizes and ages.

- Latoya McFarley is a pretty, warm honey complexion, heavy-set

African American woman, probably around 45-years-old; she was 5'5" and 260 pounds with short, light-brown hair. I met her my third day in the shelter and noted she has an intellectual disability; she is as sweet as she can be and one of my favorites. Latoya is very friendly and outgoing and likes to go walking; however, when we do take walks, we can't go too far because she runs out-of-breath quickly due to her weight. Latoya has a boyfriend named Derrick who resides in a different men's shelter in the city; I never met Derrick. They plan on using their vouchers to get an apartment together and are thinking about having a baby once they have their own place. When Latoya smiles, it's like a kid opening presents on Christmas.

Once I caught the bus with Latoya for one of her doctor's appointments, as she was being put on a new medication and didn't understand why. The following week Latoya let me know she was going to the Special Olympics on Saturday and asked if I wanted to come along. I was delighted to join her and said, yes of course, and we had a ball! I really enjoyed seeing the all the young kids and adults having such a great time with all the games and festivities. I always had a weakness for Down Syndrome kids. They are so sweet, and kind; they are really special to me!

- Then there is Deana Jenkins, a 37-year-old, tall woman at 5'11" and about 185 pounds, with toffee skin and rather plain-looking. She is an African American woman. Deana is the oldest of five children, and she has been hooked on crack cocaine for the past seventeen years. She has no significant other or children. Deana has been homeless for the past twenty years and has been in this shelter alone six times. She had a good life growing up, until her father died of cancer. A few years after that, her mother got remarried to an evil man who began molesting her until Deana ran away at the age of 17. (You see, that's something my mother never truly understood—how devastating and forever life-changing *'molestation'* can be.)

- Dorothy Hunter is a 5'4" Caucasian woman and weighs about 265 pounds. Dorothy has pale skin that always looks unwashed. Her skin sags from aging, along with permanent scarring on the left side of her face and neck, where she was severely burned when the car caught on fire. Despite her imperfections, you can see she was a beautiful woman in her day. Her hair is long-brown, limp, and greasy-looking due to the fact she barely washes it. The whole time I was there, I probably saw Dorothy leave the shelter to walk outside three times. And one of those times wasn't even optional—because one of the new girls brought in bed bugs—and they had to close down the shelter and have it fumigated so 'everybody' had to go outside. The managers did open up the cafeteria so we would have a place to sit while it was being debugged.

Being so obese, Dorothy wobbles when she walks, even with her special walker, which has tennis balls attached to the bottom to make it glide easier. Dorothy was in a car accident two years earlier, along with her husband and two kids. A drunk driver hit them and killed her entire family on impact. That caused her to have a mental breakdown from which she never recovered, and she suffers from severe depression and has been homeless ever since. She is diabetic, and her glucose levels are always running high. Dorothy gravitated to me right away. With all the deaths Dorothy was forced to endure the last few years—the complete loss of her family—she had pretty much given up on life, and that is how she ended up in the shelter.

-Next is Jasmine Nelson, very fair complexion, 19-year-old Caucasian woman with freckles and green eyes. She is 5'6" and weighs about 180 pounds with long, frizzy red hair. Jasmine, who is six months pregnant, is highly addicted to methamphetamine and does tricks for a living. She only dates African American men. Jasmine and her boyfriend lived together for about six months until their apartment caught fire while they were making meth. They broke up after they lost the apartment.

- Torrie Labelle is 5'5" and 180 pounds, with a beautiful dark espresso complexion and pretty white teeth. Torrie has short brown hair, but she wears wigs a lot, and she has plenty of them. The first day I was there, I watched Torrie change her hairstyle three times. I was so entertained; I knew we were going to get along. Torrie loves to shop online and buy things for herself and for the women in the shelter, even when she can't afford it. She always tries to look out for people she considers her friends. I told her how I felt about that, but it didn't stop her. Torrie loves to laugh, crack jokes, and have a good time. She ended up homeless after she gave up on life after the deaths of her mother, daughter, and boyfriend back-to-back. Torrie spiraled into a major depression, and it continues to be a daily struggle.

- Elizabeth Benson is olive complexioned, heavy-set, 56-year-old Caucasian woman with brown eyes and curly, unkempt short hair. She stands 5'5" and weighs 250 pounds. She does not like to shower that often, which causes a lot of problems with the other ladies. Elizabeth is plagued with major medical issues. She is morbidly obese, diabetic, has mental issues, and walks with a cane because of her two bad knees. Every first of the month, Elizabeth receives her Social Security check and food stamps, and *'every single time'* she overeats until she gets sick, and occasionally she shits on the bathroom floor. No one can prove it, but most of the women think she is the one.

- Ms. Elizabeth is a widower and became homeless a few months after her husband died. She has two sons, Jerry and Michael. Jerry, the oldest, has nothing to do with her; she calls him a ladies' man. However, she says he is more worried about the ladies than her; her youngest son Michael is a thief who is in-and-out of jail. And like clockwork, every time the first of the month rolls around, Michael calls his mother, begging for money, and eventually she gives in and gives him what he wants. Ms. Elizabeth is one of my favorites. One day, as I was watching TV in the dayroom, Ms. Elizbeth approached and decided she wanted to walk to the store. I tell her to give me a second to change my shoes, and I will walk with her. I didn't like it when the older ladies walked alone; it was dangerous in and outside the shelter.

- Then we have Rhonda Little, a 30-year-old African American woman, who grew up in foster care in Texas. Rhonda is gorgeous with a deep ebony complexion. She stands around 5'4" and weighs about 160 pounds. The lady wears nothing but beautiful, bright colors that make her stand out. She has a five-year-old daughter with a Caucasian man named John whom she met while she was living in the park. John took her home and verbally, mentally, and physically abused her. According to Rhonda, he ran over her with a car and broke her leg in two places. Their daughter Tania has been in foster care since she was two; per Rhonda, the child was born out of rape, that's how she got pregnant. I asked her why she didn't call the police and have him arrested. She laughed and said, "For what? I have been raped twelve times in foster care; what am I supposed to do? Call the cops every time? " I looked at Rhonda with laser focus and said, "Yes, Rhonda, 'every time' you are violated, you should report it." Rhonda replied that she was given hush money for being repeatedly raped by a counselor in a group home; as a result, she became pregnant and had an abortion at the age of 15.

- There is Maria Gonzales, a beautiful, voluptuous 28-year-old Hispanic woman who stands about 5'4" and weighs around 175 pounds. Her medium-length brown hair is thick and lustrous and bounces and blows in the wind, just like her personality. Maria is sweet as can be and will give you the shirt off her back. She was born the third of six siblings and had a normal childhood until the age of 15, when she became rebellious, and started running away. Hanging out with the wrong crowd began her downfall. She started drinking and experimenting with drugs.

Maria told me the story about what happened the day before her 16th birthday. She was driving her friend's 2017 Silver Nissan Maxima to pick up some Percocet pills from her drug distributor/connection; she had been popping pills and drinking all day long waiting for the call. About two hours later the call came; she left to meet up with the person and ran through a red light and killed a 35-year-old married Caucasian woman, the mother of 4. The woman died on impact. Maria was sentenced to ten years for involuntary manslaughter. She spent seven years in prison, and once she was released, she was doing well for a while; she became an assistant manager at Sonic's fast-food restaurant and had her own apartment. Unfortunately, her demons came back, and she began to drink and take pills, eventually graduating to the hard stuff—heroin. It wasn't long before she lost everything and began prostituting for her fix.

Lisa is estranged from her family, who she says are all successful. She has been in and out of shelters for a few years now, but I am proud to say she has been clean for 4 months.

The one thing most of the women had in common was that they trusted me enough that every month when they received their Social Security checks, I would take their debit cards with their pin numbers in hand and walk to the bank to withdraw whatever amount they needed. They would always offer me money; usually I wouldn't take it. I had a few friends and family members that always made sure I had money. I was good.

Daily we have a curfew to be inside the building by 8:00 PM, and it's lights out at 10:30 PM. On the weekends, we are allowed to stay up until 11:30 PM. This is usually when the crazy shit starts; people are outside drinking and getting high, and before you know it, a fight breaks out. (You see, The Shelter has no jurisdiction over what happens 'outside the shelter,' only inside, and trust me, the residents take full advantage.)

- Regina Hughes, the 65-year-old African American alcoholic, who comes in drunk as usual every night. I don't think I have ever seen her sober, to be honest. She has been at this shelter off and on for the past 10 years. Regina is about 5'9" and at 130 pounds is very skinny. She had a pretty toffee complexion with big brown doe eyes to match. She always spoke with her two sons often. Unfortunately, shortly after the incident with her and Elizabeth, which follows, she was kicked out of the shelter due to her unruly, drunken behavior. About a month later, she died of alcohol poisoning.

Regina had a serious issue with Ms. Elizabeth (the widower who overeats and has the son that is always begging whenever she receives her Social Security check), and I have no idea how this conflict between them started. Tonight, Regina decides to blast her music without using her earphones, which really starts to get on Ms. Elizabeth's nerves. Ms. Elizabeth screams at Regina, "Turn that shit down!!" Ms. Regina answers her with a piercing screech, "You're just mad 'cause *you ain't got shit to eat!!*" Ms. Frances starts barking decibels louder, *"They don't ever do shit to her drunk ass; it's because I'm white!!!"*

By now, three or four more women have joined the growing fray. Gloria catapults up and yells, "I'm calling 911; this isn't right! Leave Ms. Elizabeth alone!" Regina jumps up, screaming in her face, "You sound just like a plantation owner! Shut your ass up!!!" It has become an "all-out race war." Now, we have about three security guards finally racing in trying to intervene. After about another 30 minutes of shrieking, and howling, and screeching back and forth between both groups, it is finally settled, and everyone calms down. (No doubt they just wore their lungs out and have no more breath left to holler!) That night I go to sleep covering my head and thinking, 'What in the hell have I gotten myself into?'

By the way, when they were not at each other's throats, all these women, including myself, kept our facility in tip-top shape. We all switched off-and-on specific job duties every other week or so: cleaning the dayroom, the front office and reception area, the shower room with 5 or 6 stalls, and the lavatory area, which had individual toilet stalls. It's pretty amazing—women who had hit the bottom of the barrel—strangers living in very close quarters, fighting and scamming, yet we kept our living quarters clean. There was a certain culture and communal standards that ruled The Shelter that weren't necessarily in the handbook. This was our "Home," collectively. I was a sort of leader—not arrogant or pushy—but as a human being who truly cared about them. They could tell I was genuine.

After dinner, most of the ladies hung out in the dayroom watching TV, playing cards, or listening/talking on their phones. I recall one night watching TV sitting beside Deana; next to her were Torrie and Brenda, and suddenly, Maria walked up to me. I immediately noticed she had her hair straightened out—unlike her naturally curly-textured hair she normally wears—and I said, "Maria, your hair looks so beautiful." Maria responded in such a calm voice, "Thank you. You know that bitch Deana stole my shower shoes and two of my scratch-off tickets." I look at Maria and at Deana; then I look back at Maria while pointing to Deana and say, "Who, her?" Maria raised her head, "Yeah, that bitch." At once, Deana starts screaming at Maria.

What the fuck?? It was time to exit. Nope, I didn't want any part of that shit, so I picked up my purse and walked my ass right outside. - It was about an hour later before I came back inside. The girls were separated, but they were still arguing back and forth. I went in the back, took my shower, and lay on my bed. I started thinking about my own life, and all the other girls' fiascos faded into the background… they were dealing with their own shit. But here in my own space, I realized this is the first time I actually had *peace in my life:* no bills, no stress, no family, no partner. I hit the basement of hell but finally felt free. -- What did that say about me? I became a little frightened at that thought. Was my life that chaotic and fragmented that I actually had to leave every single piece behind—my marriage, my house, my family, my money, my job, my husbands—and fall straight to the abyss of hell before I could finally have peace within?? I feel like I'm in an alternative universe... strange, but it feels right and good.

At one point, I go back on the Taimi lesbian dating site. Scrolling around, I start talking to a few ladies just as friends, nothing more, nothing less. As far as the job situation goes, I've had two interviews so far, both receptionist jobs. I didn't get either one. I am a little 'down,' but I know sooner or later it will happen.

Early one Saturday morning, Maria and I decided to catch the bus to Walmart to buy some personal things and grab some lunch to make a day of it. I remember we found everything we needed at Walmart. Maria bought some make-up and eyelashes. I was running out of a few items, so I bought my Cantu shea butter shampoo and conditioner, Jergens Ultra Healing lotion, and Olay Ultra Moisturizing body wash. They do give out free sample sizes of personal hygiene items in The Shelter, but I prefer what I am used to. After a delightful day of shopping, we walked across the parking lot to TGI Fridays for lunch. Maria ordered the Cobb salad with a sweet tea, and I had a chicken Caesar salad with lemonade, and for dessert I had the Brownie Obsession. I have a really bad sweet tooth. Honestly, I think I eat more desserts than food. The 'Brownie

Obsession' *is* an obsession—a scrumptious chocolate brownie with a big scoop of vanilla bean ice cream, drizzled with caramel sauce and topped with glazed pecans. Wow, it was amazing! We really enjoyed ourselves.

On the way back to the shelter we had to wait for our second bus to arrive, which was due in about 10 minutes. We sat on the bench; it was a little crowded, and I remember saying to Maria, "I will be so glad when we get back to The Shelter so I can take a shower and relax." Immediately the young African American man who was sitting beside me looked over at me and turned his nose up, as if I was trash. He got up and walked to the opposite side of the bench; watching him I said to Maria, "I guess he thought I was going to get shelter germs on him."

When we got back to The Shelter, I immediately took a shower, changed clothes and sat on my bunk. I could feel the depression start to creep in; it was the first time I felt humiliated since I'd been here. I immediately went to YouTube on my phone, put my headphones on and turn to my faithful Funky Dineva and just play random videos of him discussing what he does when he gets into a deep depressive state and how he deals with it. Boy, I really don't know what I would do without his videos during these times. He truly was a Lifesaver!

Well, time was moving on and the seasons were changing. The scent and warmth of summer were in the air, and on the 10th of June 2023, I Bella, turned 50 years old while in The Samantha B. Brown Shelter. It was sad, I won't lie. But I bought myself the best gift I could give myself, an AARP membership card. I know eventually I will be back into society so I will need my discounts. Despite it all, I have a very practical side to me, which in many cases has been an asset. I made it to 50 in this world, that is an accomplishment in itself, especially considering the life I have been living the last few months. I have a new dream with my new milestone, my "50th Birthday," and that is, one day I hope to be a spokesperson for AARP! Many of the younger ladies couldn't believe my age and hope that they look like me when they make it to 50.

Summer was a fortuitous season for me and on July 10th, I got the call I've been waiting so long for—it was a call-back for an interview from KEK Glass, a national company. When I go to the appointment, *I ace the interview, and I am hired!* It's a call center Customer Care position working in the Corporate department, and it's a work from home position. I have a laptop with me but I 'cannot work' out of the shelter. This was my big cue – time for a brand-new Leaf...so I packed my belongings and prepared to leave. – I said my goodbyes to everyone and gave extra hugs to my favorites. I wished them "All" the best of luck and meant it.

It's an interesting thing about this "Shelter Life. "—There wasn't a welcoming committee when I walked in, and there wasn't a bon voyage committee upon leaving. The Shelter is like a "Way Station," a place where you *'wait,'* until you find out where Life is going to lead you next. For some of these ladies, it's right back through the door. But for each lady I met, they meant something. We had all fallen into hell – we were all in the same war. I take a part of each of them with me, a part of their unbelievable lives that they all shared with me. They are part of me now...my own journey—we went to battle and ended up in this place. As I close this Shelter door, I leave the same way I came—in an Uber—but one major thing has changed forever more—Me. I fell into the deepest pit of hell and with mates that made the same journey. Thanks to God, Granny and Myself, I made the first step out... A New Life awaits me. I think I am beginning to sow my 1st seeds in my own Garden.

Chapter 12

The Sun Shines Through ~ "Transformation—Resolutions"

There was no pause after The Shelter door closed behind me; I looked forward and kept walking. It was like leaving the bottomless pit of hell where I had fallen unceremoniously on my ass. But I was immediately on to the next step, the next stage of my life. I got into the waiting Uber with never a backward glance. I had chosen to dig my nails in and climb out of that devastating abyss. Now, I was taking the first step of my New Life, instructing the driver without hesitation, "Please take me to the closest Extended Stay Hotel."

Granted, the hotel is not 5 stars, or 4, or even a 3-star lodge, but it's damn sure better than living in a shelter. And the most wonderful thing was—I would start my new job with KEK Glass on July 17th just a few days later. (I had a thought—how ironic it was that I was working for a glass company. Me, who had shattered glass into a million pieces. Now, I was going to help others repair and restore their broken glass. – Poor glass had nothing to do with it… God works in mysterious ways to help us learn lessons from our own misdirected rage.) In any event—onward. The new job left me happy but broke; I bring home $465.00; after taxes every week, my weekly rate stay is $417.00, which leaves me only $48. I have been in the hotel for about six months now—unable to save any money—but being out of the shelter is a blessing of its own. I continue to talk to a few ladies from the dating site, and one particular day I end up chatting with a lady I shall call Madison McClain. She is a Gemini too, and we get along so well. We met up and hung out a few times, and then Madison offered me a place to stay; I would split the bills with her. God is good. What a blessing! I immediately said "yes."

On January 19, 2024, I moved into Madison's apartment, and can I tell you what a harmonious, mentally stable environment felt like?? It was heaven! After years of these cataclysmic events in my life—following me around like a tortuous storm cloud that could erupt at a moment's notice and turn into a vicious hurricane—these emotionally healthy surroundings were like nourishing oxygen tanks feeding my soul. I finally started to feel alive and human again. But let's be real and honest. I also know I needed therapy for *everything* I have been through. So, I made an appointment with a 57-year-old African American female therapist named Charlene Baker who is part of the LGBT+ community; that is specifically why I chose her.

On March 9, 2024, I had my first Zoom consultation with Charlene, which consisted mainly of answering questions. We discussed my background a little bit, and I let her know I had been living in a shelter for about three months. Charlene seemed intrigued and asked if I had ever been to jail. I answered, "Yes, I worked in a prison for eight years." She then asked if I had ever been to a drug and rehabilitation center. "Yes, in 2019 for alcoholism," I replied. (This is the one place you don't have to hide anything.) After about an hour, our session concluded. I thanked her and told her I looked forward to seeing her in two weeks.

My second appointment with Ms. Baker took place on March 23, 2024. We began our session by exchanging pleasantries, *but* I am ready to get down to business. We talk, but it's more like talking to a friend. I am telling her my life story, and though I feel she is listening to me, I am not getting any advice or home assignments to do. It was a disappointment. I spoke with my roommate Madison and told her I always thought about writing a book about my life. Maybe that was also a form of therapy. She responded positively, "Why not? You are definitely a vibe."

I was fortunate to find and meet a kindred soul as my writer. In many ways, it was like going to therapy. Because Arista is so calming and nonjudgmental, I wanted to tell her more things. The journey of writing this book was a profound experience that categorized and organized my life, so I can see better where I have been. It was like entering a world where I could safely share my secrets and reveal things I could never really discuss before. I recommend this process of self-discovery to anyone, even if you're just jotting down notes or keeping a journal. It will benefit you in ways you've never imagined—taking a journey through your entire life that you may not have acknowledged before...because it was just too painful. On March 24, 2024, I started on my autobiography. The main goal—"If I can just stop 'one person' from making any of the mistakes I made in my life, I will feel like I have made a difference."

"Child Molestation"

In the closing chapters, I'd like to share with you a major part of what I have learned *'because of and through my life's journey.'* I hope it will inspire and encourage anyone who has faced or is facing deeply affecting issues such as 'Child Molestation,' 'Family Dysfunction,' 'Mental, Physical, and Emotional Abuse,' and 'Generational Addiction.'

The child molestation my cousin perpetrated on me when I was 5—little more than a baby—took my innocence. It was life-changing, and due to that traumatic event, I have never been able to sleep on my back since the day it happened. If you remember, I once had a conversation with my mother about it. I bared my soul and told her, "The only thing I pray for is that I'll be able to sleep on my back before I die." I nearly begged her to go to therapy with me– and her response was, "No, all they do is blame the momma; I drank to get over it."

Now that I think about it, 'Why was it always about her...and not me? I was the child. She was supposed to protect me.' When she refused to support me as a little girl and told me to pretend it never happened—tell no one in the family—that not only broke my heart but broke the hope of ever having a real, trusting relationship with my mother. And severing that hope permanently is when they rubbed salt into the wound by inviting him (my cousin who did the deed) to family holiday parties. I remember questioning my mother, *"What is going on?"* She responded smugly, *"Well, you run around laughing—you musta liked it."* After I recovered from that gut punch, I started to tell my grandmother, but I knew she would have cussed my mother out. And Granny didn't even cuss. But I told my mother that day, "You're a sick bitch. You may be my mother, but I do not like you." Looking back, I was too kind with my words…"

Since the age of 5, when I was violated, I have 'literally' not been able to sleep on my back. Nearing my 51st birthday, it is only now in Madison's safe haven that I can once again sleep on my back. … And yet, I still sleep with my hands over my vagina; that is "my protector." For 45 straight years, my mind would automatically tell me, "You've got to sleep on your side, Bella, not on your back, because you're going to be touched." … So, when people say, "Oh, Bill Cosby raped her twenty years ago. That was twenty years ago." It never goes away for years. They don't understand. Your mind never forgets and keeps playing that tape over and over again—until you are ready, willing, and able to press "Stop." (It is a long, complex journey for most of us, but worth every single step that leads to—"STOP!")

It was in rehab that I probably took my first step. There, I learned so much about myself—how child molestation can change the way you think, feel, say, and do for the rest of your life. It's universal—families sweeping it under the carpet—but I'm so glad it's changing. I hope that they are checking on the boys too—all those little boys that are being/have been abused. Nobody's safe from a predator. Take that infamous person who had a lock on his office door, committing violation after violation against women, threatening his victims with their careers they had worked all their lives to build. And if they didn't bend *(literally)* to his sick commands, he would make sure they never worked in their industry again! The powers that be allowed this to happen for years.

Later in therapy, I would learn that even though "sure, you'd like to forget it," your mind has been programmed, and that becomes your 'normal,' when it is truly *abnormal.* That is "why" rehab and professional counseling are so important and helpful in guiding you to open up and discover who you are, find out what's behind and beneath the issues that have plagued you all your life, and implement therapy that will assist you in resolving these life-altering traumas. Remember, these services are often covered by insurance, offer sliding-scale payment structures, and are even available to homeless individuals in rehab facilities and shelters. You may not find the perfect therapist for yourself the first time but keep trying; you will learn something from each one, even if it's one sentence that stays with you, one memory that shines a light on something you didn't want to see. Professional counseling is an essential component in the healing process.

"Family Dysfunction"

In today's world, if you did a search on the latest statistics of "Dysfunctional Families," there would be a high percentage of us who experienced and grew up in a 'broken environment' often perpetuating that culture throughout our lives. I know in my own life, I've witnessed it happening in all walks of life: from homeless to millionaires, junkies to CEOs, walking on the streets, at work, at church, and in the prisons I worked.

The one thing I do know is "it all starts at home." The parents, the family, the relatives, the friends, the culture we grow up in our neighborhood, school, and community—it all contributes to who we become and what kind of individual garden we will cultivate. The first people we interact with become our influencers, who shape how we think, who we learn to trust (or not), and who we want to be. Through them, we define what we want in life and how to get it.

As a child, I can recall many good times I had with friends and school. But sometimes these happy moments are overshadowed by unforgettable events, such as the time I was 6 and came home from school to find my mother all bloody, passed out on the floor, with liquor bottles, and a straight razor nearby. You haven't the slightest idea what's going on; all you know is you have to run for help and keep your wits about you because suddenly you're having trouble breathing (at 6 years old) and the words are coming out jumbled. Then, there's a whole block of time when you are without a mother: Where'd she go? Here one day, gone for months, and then shows up one day as spontaneously as she disappeared. And now you are living with your "Granny" in another state—going back and forth, and back and forth. This becomes your "normal." You are 3 feet tall, and you just do what you're told. Sometimes you feel like you're all by yourself. You don't have a father, a *what?* What's that—a "father"? It's never talked about; there are no pictures of any fathers anywhere in your house, even though two brothers come into your life. That is a picture of my "Dysfunctional Family."

But then you come to realize you are not alone. There is a "Heroine of Everything," your GRANNY. — She is the Grandmother, Mother and Father, Mentor, and the only Trusted and Respected Adult Figure in your life. I learned early on who the "head' of our family was—my Granny. She was my "Everything" because, let's be honest, my mother was who she was, and my father wasn't even around, so he definitely wasn't shit; Papa was a rollin' stone. He had a baby...and another...and another, and just kept movin'—leaving behind every child he sired. That was 'my father,' a prototype of "Generational Male Behavior and Entitlement." (Men could do everything they wanted to do, even in 2024. In Punjab, there were 300+ honor killings against women. Just because a sister was engaging in "online dating"—her brother was able to kill her. Finally, after centuries of condoning such crimes, men are being prosecuted, and true honor is being restored. In a *Dateline* episode, men would come to the U.S. from these countries and kill their daughters in the name of their primitive code of honor. But guess what? "Here," you are going to be prosecuted. We're not perfect, but we have evolved...

The two most important influences in your life are your "mother" and "father." They can affect and influence your life—all your life. "Who Do You Trust?" I think it comes down to analyzing, dissecting, and being brutally honest with yourself about who they are and why they are the way they are, and hopefully in time come to a place where you can offer understanding, compassion, and forgiveness. Sometimes, if they continue to hurt and abuse you, you may have to contemplate moving completely away from them, living without them—but from a place of love. You too have a God-given right to live and be happy. No commandment says you must be a doormat or punching bag or hang on a cross for 'their sins'.

Let's take the first significant person in your life, "the Mother." Honestly, finding my mother all bloodied when I was 6, and later, when I was older, learning "she did do drugs," was the primary reason I never "did drugs myself." —I knew my mother Bridgette was doing heroin, though I never saw her do it, but it made me say to myself, "I will never do anything stronger than marijuana." My mother nipped that potential addiction in the bud when I saw what it did to her. Even as a child, though I didn't understand about drugs, I knew if my mother was weak, I could be weak and fall prey to these addictions. Although I was weak-minded in other things, I *'was not'* when it came to doing drugs. Years later, in Rehab in 2019, the therapist diagnosed me as being "too independent," which makes sense. They said the reason is because, at a young age, when I was hurt, I realized I had no one to go to, which is 100% correct, and therefore I won't let anyone help me. I will go "without" before I ask for help. I will work 2 or 3 jobs. Now, I feel like "I am here for me—*I have to be here for me.*"

But despite getting hurt time and time again, you still "reach out" when you want and need your mother—the need for a mother-daughter relationship must be hard-wired. Take the time I was going to marry Kevin; my mother was adamant, "No, no, you can't!" Well, you can hear that till you're blue in the face, but "Love is love." The truth is, you're the one who has to get hurt enough to say, "Okay, this is enough. I'm not doing this anymore. Let me STOP!" What my mother was doing was not helping but hurting me. In trying to break us up along with Kevin doing dirt to me, it actually had the opposite effect; it was pushing us closer together. She was just adding fuel to the fire. I'm twenty-two years old, and it's my mother who is riding up and down the road looking for Kevin because she heard he was beating on me or cheating on me. – It just wasn't necessary.

Bridgette made matters worse by not understanding I loved Kevin, whereas she hated him. The truth of the matter is—my mother hated Kevin more than anything—because he was like looking into a mirror. He reminded "her of herself" when she was in the streets as an addict. It was that, and putting his hands on me was what she hated. Other than that, she could care less about me, as you can see in this book. It was her hatred toward him that was her driving force—he was an arrogant drug dealer. My Aunt Joan tried to clarify it for me. She said Kevin was not only a drug dealer, but he was also a 'very good fighter.' He had quite a name in the streets: "You don't try him, 'cause he could knock you out." She explained further, "Back in the day, your mother had the same reputation. You didn't mess with your mother; she was in those streets too." Thank God for our grandmother (her mother), who brought that other light into our lives. We would have been walking around flailing in the darkness otherwise.

As Bridgette was about the streets too, you had two people that lived the same kind of lifestyle trying to control the same person—Me! They were going to battle. Kevin controlled me, and when he wasn't controlling me, my mother was. One time I was about 25 years old and was living in my own home when my Granny called me and said, "I need to talk to you." Right away, I drove down to Bridgette's house where Granny was living and my cousin, Marcus (my Aunt Joan's son), was there, and I said to him, "What did I do wrong? Granny called, and she said she needed to talk to me. What did I do?" Marcus looked at me and shook his head. "You fool. You're twenty-five years old with your own house. What are you worried about if you did something wrong??" But, you see, all my family had that kind of mentality when it came to me, "What did they hear? Did Kevin cheat on me? Did I do this, did I do that?" They were like a bunch of crows pickin' at me. I didn't know where to turn with all this babble in my head.

I had to completely lose everything, including my house, to get away from ALL of it. — I had to go to a homeless shelter with other homeless strangers, so I could think by "myself," *hear* myself think, and not hear a hundred voices pointing fingers at me. It took going to The Shelter to get my head straight, with no one there but me—no bills, no worries, no one calling me (because none of my family knew where I was). Sometimes, folks, you have to free yourself from everyone and everything, including your family, to find yourself and hear your own damn voice. Then, you can see a picture of your own life clearly...without any interference, pressure, or weight pulling you down. It took me to hit damn rock bottom to finally find and feel 'peace.'

To be fair, my mother helped with the material things: a roof over our heads, food, and things we wanted to do in school—not more, not less—but the thing I needed and wanted most she could not give me, "Love." "You didn't show me the love I was dying for; you didn't correct my behaviors; you didn't help me or get help 'to fix me.' And when I was 5, I needed you to defend, protect, and support me. Refusing to go to therapy with me because "I" needed it, not because it made you drink. Not beating me like a man because I wouldn't clean the bathroom and told you to clean it yourself. I was 15 years old, and the next thing I knew, you punched me in the side of my face near my temple, and I landed in the bathtub, and you didn't stop at just one; you repeatedly pounded me. All I could do was put my hands up against my face like a boxer, trying to block every punch you threw. (I had to defend myself from "you.") I remember it took my Granny, cousin Marcus, and brother Brandon to finally pull you off me." My dislike turned to hate for my mother that day. And now that I think more about it, "Who was my mother really beating so violently that day she couldn't stop?" ... There were so many of Bridgette's behaviors that were uncalled for and undealt with. To hear my mother tell it, "I didn't physically abuse you—'you *had a great life.'* I didn't beat you; you had food." Yeah, you fed me all right, but funny how you forgot you 'beat me like a man' when I was 15... over cleaning a damn bathroom.

Yes, regarding my mother, there were many empty holes that remained unfilled. I offer forgiveness; I do... but forgetting is much harder. We have no communication, the bare minimum. To be honest, Bridgette and I don't really have a relationship. I know there is a therapy in which you write out all the things you want to say—the unspoken words and offenses, the hurts that are still with you 45 years later, and even if you don't, or can't mail, or give it to the person, the point is you bared your soul and wrote it. You can lay out the words on paper and see them clearly instead of just letting them poison and hurt your insides. Then you bless them with love and blow them gently away like the fluff on a dandelion. And with renewed hope, you can open your heart to a different kind of love from a different source…a different person…and be happy for the road that led you there.

As for my father, Michael St. Patrick, well, that's a few short paragraphs. Remember, I never laid eyes on the man until I was 23 years old, and only then to meet a half-sister who was dying from alcoholism. The next time my father and I met, it should have been a proud and happy occasion because one of his 3 daughters—"me"—had bought and built her own house at the tender age of 25! But, sadly by then, I had joined the 'generational alcohol addiction,' introduced by my dying beautiful half-sister: "Lemon Drops with Seagram's Gin." So, when my father came to visit me for two weeks at my house, we made it a two-week drinking binge holiday. He drank his Bud Light beer and ate his potato chips. He loves any and every flavor or brand of potato chips, and I drank my Seagram's Gin straight out of the bottle. I will say this—my father made the best-deviled eggs with the perfect amount of paprika and dill relish; it had just enough bitterness. So pretty much that's what we ate and drank the entire two weeks he stayed with me. To be honest, never having a father, especially one who only called me once a year on my birthday, I really didn't miss not having a dad so much—except in school when we had to put our family tree together—that sucked. Also, as I've mentioned, "Granny" was our Mother, Father, Grandmother, and Grandfather. She was a One-for-All.

And for whatever reason, I understood my father Michael's inability to '*become attached to anyone or anything*' because his mother died giving birth to him. I related to that quality because I think I have that part of him in me too. Maybe that explains why our father was too afraid to get close to any of his daughters. And to be fair, my father did agree that I could come live with him when I was running away from my mother, who lied to me and stopped me from going. Though I can't help but wonder: Would he have kept me had I gone to live with him? Would it have been a happier, more stable life? Who knows? Maybe I did give my father more of a pass than my mother, but that's because Bridgette had a very good mother and stepfather. My father never had a mom. Life is hard to untangle—at least my *broken tree* is!

I recently spoke to my father's sister because no one knew where he was. Sometimes he goes missing for months. They couldn't find him in Tallahassee, Florida, so my dad's sister went on Facebook looking for me. She got in touch with me, but I told her I hadn't spoken to my father in a couple years. She gave me his phone number so I could have it. I did leave my dad a message, but I'm not sure it went through; his phone might be disconnected. Michael has been an alcoholic and has had problems with it off and on throughout his life. Sad to say, I think he's back drinking—heavy.

For my father, I wish him well too. There's really nothing to let go of; it will always be a hole because there was nothing ever planted there. It's easy to say, "It is what it is; your mother and father were what they were and are what they are." But when you are talking about the two people in your life who are the most influential, those words become heavy and weigh on your soul. For me, it is pulling off all the covers, getting to know who each of my parents is, where and what they came from, what they are capable of and not, bringing it all out in the open, and exposing the hidden feelings making you sick inside. You see it; you feel the pain and the MIAs (missing in action); acknowledge the abuse and the missing love and support. Then you mourn it, accept what it is if it can't be changed, and eventually move on. Every step is like dragging your feet through cement because that damn baggage can be so heavy (especially after carrying it so long), but I have found if you deal with each piece, the load gets lighter and you can throw it off. The challenge is not to go back and retrieve it again—out of habit, victimization, or acculturation. *Keep going and looking forward.*

Forgiveness and compassion are good (hate and vengeance we know only rot your insides), and don't let anyone hurt you. Be your own parent, protect, and defend yourself. Love and support yourself. If they don't want to, can't better themselves, or get the help they need, that's their choice. We got enough to work on ourselves, right? For me, I consider myself very fortunate, for if I didn't have the parents I needed, I had surrogate parents in my grandmother. I always leaned on my grandmother. Outside of that, I let them ride. Granny was My Rock all day long.

I truly hope you can find your own Granny, even if it's yourself. I share again with you my Granny's last words when I told her, "I'll never make it without you." She responded, "You're strong, Bella; you'll make it without me." Granny had faith in me—but just as importantly, now *I have faith in me.* - And *I have faith in you, each of you,* because we truly are our brothers' and sisters' keepers. We're all on this complex, interactive journey together. No man is an island. All that stuff begins to make sense when you get out of your head, and in my case, put it down on paper.

"Partner—Mental, Physical, and Emotional Abuse"

Let me tell you again another reason why I cut Kevin so much slack. He came from a small country town. You have two clubs—The Club Palace and The Pale Diamond—which constitute your entire world of entertainment and social activity. Whoopee! The people born and raised there—most never left. They never leave the entire state of New Jersey! There are other states to explore, but they couldn't get past the state boundaries. They never experienced life outside of their own enforced perimeter; that's all they know. I came back into this environment after I had become a teenager, so I knew better; I had experienced life outside these fences. These are just some small-town country people. I'm not saying pity them; just try to understand where they came from. This is where their gardens grew and those roots go deep—generations and generations. ...Maybe, that's what Kevin was doing, shining as bright as he could in his little plot of land.

And I guess I could never get that picture of Kevin's mother out of my head. You know if the husband is abusing the wife, he's probably doing it to the children too. However, as I got older, I felt what his mother did was a copout; yet years later, the kids would talk to her. It kind of made me realize why Kevin was putting his hands on me; that's what he saw growing up, and that's what's accepted in these little rural towns. If a man beats his wife, that's their business. We don't get involved. Back then, that's how it was, and in many ways it still is.

But today women have empowered themselves by building their own careers and lives, and most importantly, themselves. They are changing the trajectory by raising their sons in a different culture—to respect women and support them and their children. It is becoming a different world, a different garden, different seeds growing men who value equality. They see the beauty and intelligence of women and don't fear it but can celebrate it. They are more secure in themselves and are evolving past physical and mental abuse, as women are discovering and empowering themselves and refusing to 'be victims.' That's a mighty transformation. Sure, this is the 'ideal state,' but that's what we're creating by changing our thoughts and throwing out the old tapes. The "old state of mind" is what kept me paralyzed.

In one way, I think Kevin's mom was an early pioneer; she finally got fed up with the chronic abuse and just up and left. However, she *didn't* take the kids with her, which the mother would have normally done. ...I'm sorry... You don't just leave your children to the abuser.

How do *you get away yourself* and say, "Well, I'm okay, but he's gonna beat my kids to death." What kind of—I don't know... Kevin and his sister and brother were all abandoned. (I knew them all; we laughed and played together.) It was no secret their father used to beat their mother. There were 3 of them—Tameka, then Kevin, followed by Trevor, the youngest brother. When Trevor was about two years old, his father got mad at his mother and took the two-year-old into the woods. He left the baby there, came back home, and said to the mother, "You go get him." Their mother left the next morning, went to Alabama, and never returned. She was so scared of that man; she didn't want any part of him anymore. But my problem with that is—so you left your kids with a maniac.—*That's* my problem! So, basically, Kevin is a total product of his environment—he didn't have love. It was his aunt who actually raised him and his siblings.

And that's why people take the paths they do, and that's why I try to understand why people end up being where they are—*'especially after my time in that shelter.'* I comprehend that you can't stand there and see your mother being beaten time after time and no one is saying or doing anything, and your mother just accepts it and *acts like it's all right.*—That's what a lot of women still do and children haven't a clue or the power yet to do anything.

Because of the way I was raised, I didn't suffer that kind of abuse and wasn't witness to it. I was blessed because the two-parent home to me was my grandmother and mother. Men have been doing whatever they want since the beginning of time. It happens in every race. It's our life; you either roll with the punches or lay down. It's universal—in all families—African American, Caucasian, Hispanic, and Asian sweep molestation/rape/abuse under the carpet. Or worse, the women are not believed and the men are not blamed for the abuse; it's so sick. The devil is beating his wife! It's acceptable to this day in many small country towns and villages, all over the world.

After Kevin and I experienced our sweet, innocent "Summer of Love," that's what I expected to find when my mother moved us back to New Jersey following my graduation from high school. But Kevin was a changed man, I found instead—a successful drug dealer sporting gold teeth as a mark of his status—some kind of badge of honor.

But, friends, "Love is the game-changer." I admit it, I was probably still in love with him—a fine-looking man; we had chemistry and history since the age of 5 when we rode the bus to school together--Kevin, me, and his siblings. We were inseparable. --And now I was living in his environment—*and for the first time in my life*—when I came home from work I looked forward to seeing Kevin. He was 'not so arrogant as he became.' We had an apartment and 'I never paid a bill.' I would come home, and Kevin would have 5 or 6 outfits laid out for me; he had gone shopping, just for me. I was 20-21 when I returned from the military, a tough immature stint I tried to make into a career. It hadn't worked out as planned, so the attention and gifts were welcome. My mother was observing the way I was living and once she confronted me (not too aggressively), "So, you don't ever want to get a job, or do anything? You just want your drug dealer boyfriend to take care of you?" I reply laughingly, "Yeah, pretty much then I did." People can get used to pretty much anything.

And you see the gifts lose their luster when your man starts the shit of generational cheating, "Oh, I treat her damn good, I give her the things she wants. - I'm *'the man.'* I can do anything I want, whenever I want to." You pay with your soul for those little niceties. But you see that's where the difference between us lies—*I am not a product of that environment*—and I'm not going to accept that kind of behavior. I was not raised that way. Somewhere inside me, my Granny had seeded 'SELF-RESPECT' by her own example. My Granny left after only one time when her 1st husband, Kenneth Williams Jr, (my grandfather, Pop Pop) put his hands on her. She wasn't going to allow "any man" to humiliate her…and neither was her granddaughter, Bella, but I had to learn the hard way. Was I still in Love or lust with Kevin? Was I still *waiting for him to change?* Did I think by loving him so much and forgiving him so much he would change?? But I learned something else. Besides my continuing compassion and understanding for the man, there was something else within that was being brutalized—MY SELF-RESPECT—and that would have severe consequences.

I learned in this small town, there was no hiding from a cheater, and what he did to you is witnessed by "Everyone in the town." And let me tell you, I did not like this feeling of humiliation and disrespect, not one bit!!! PEOPLE KNEW. Bryson's parents knew—the young autistic man I worked for on weekends. I was so distressed by that harrowing, traumatic incident when I took that hiatus from work to go look for MY CAR which was being driven BY KEVIN'S GIRLFRIEND, I nearly lost my mind. I also had to let Bryson's parents know why I wasn't coming to care for their son. It was so humiliating that everyone KNEW about "Kevin's cheating!" AND, come to find out, the girl lived in the same town. Everyone knew MY CAR, and they had seen the girl driving my car around town like it was hers. How mortifying! I had this job taking care of Bryson way before Kevin pulled this crap, and Bryson's parents always thought so highly of me! And here I am in the medical field working a respectable job, where both your colleagues and the patients '*show you respect,*' and now all my colleagues know this *low life* is 'cheating on me.' It was like being sucker punched and everyone in the whole town was witnessing it. How utterly demeaning. But not one of them looked at me like I was a fool or did something wrong. They knew it was him; their reaction was more akin to, "How did you get hooked up with this trash?"

This was the first of many traumatic events that would transpire between Kevin and me. What I did not know is every single one of them has a cost to you. They will build up until one day the pressure inside from all the lies and transgressions—and they are cumulative—like throwin' another hot coal on the fire that is already raging, and one day … it will just explode. Like a bomb. It would become the fight of my life *"for my life."* This is something I hope you can avoid by seeing the signs ahead of time. But it is as you know, 'a process.'

Kevin and I would part, sever ties, each getting on with our respective lives. Several years would pass by, maybe softening the past hurts and infractions. And Kevin is in prison, on some drug charge I think. So. I find out where he is located and start writing him again...And why in the world, you ask, would you start writing him again?? ...Because I looked at him as a friend too, and I felt sorry for him, and I always had Granny in my life, no matter what. He had been alone since the day he came onto the earth. If I was in a situation where I needed anything, I could call my Granny and say, "It's an emergency. I need $10,000; she'd have it." He never had that kind of life, so I kind of felt sorry for him, *and* quite frankly I loved him. I was 'in love with him.'

Remember this: I say it again, "LOVE" is the Gamechanger." Oftentimes, it causes one not to see the obstacles that are glaringly clear from people on the outside looking in. It causes you to think only from your heart, not your rational mind...*and* listen to nice words because that's what we want to hear. It feels good: we want to believe that *this time* when you hear, "I won't ever do those things to you again. – It was wrong. I don't need "to cheat." I'm going to be much better." And you begin to believe the man – maybe, he *is changing.* – It's worth another chance. Uh-uh, are you listening to yourself, Bella? Kevin not only looks good...he is a *very good manipulator.*

He came out of prison and it was a honeymoon for the first couple of months, then the bare-faced lies start up again... *'right to your face'*: not coming home at night, again and again, and you are a fool, *'asking him, where's he been, with who?' When you know damn well where he's been—you just can't prove it...yet.* –And to add salt to the wound, Kevin comes waltzing in the door the next morning, and announces, "Where's my breakfast?" And "you," like a dog with its tail between its legs, so defeated by his lies, listen to him *gaslightin'* and ridiculing you, "You're just crazy!" And you just make the damn breakfast and serve it to him. But mind you, the day will come, and it won't be pretty...when you'll reach through your soul and exact retribution.

-- And those "Piles of Abuses"—Mental, Physical, Emotional, and Spiritual—cumulatively gather until you have years and years of instances and instances of abuse that fester into a firestorm of retribution that eventually erupt like the Volcano of your Life. – You don't know what the hell hit you, but you "do know," It STOPS *Tonight:* TONIGHT, YOU ARE *NOT* TELLING ME ONE MORE LIE. TONIGHT, YOU ARE NOT LEAVING ME ALONE AND GOING TO YOUR BITCH. TONIGHT, YOU ARE NOT LAUGHING IN MY FACE AND CALLING ME CRAZY. –You are just a little person who has reached the point of no return, you get into Kevin's car and with all the strength of your being rise up like 'Super-Woman' and KICK THE SHIT OUT OF THE ABUSER'S WINDSHIELD, UNTIL IT SHATTERS INTO A BILLION PIECES OF BROKEN GLASS, symbolizing the YEARS OF DISRESPECT, HURT, AND LIES. TODAY, you are now willing to get your JUSTICE, even if it means YOU MURDER THE ABUSER AND GO TO PRISON FOR THE REST OF YOUR LIFE.

Oh yeah, I had it all figured out. I knew the Bastard was cheating, I KNEW he was leaving the house to meet his girlfriend so I acted a fool telling myself it's okay—I'm a rational person, I got this—"If I kill him, I'll probably only get 10 years on manslaughter." At this point, I was mentally able to take him out because it meant regaining "my entire worth" as a human being which had been beaten down to a pile of nothingness. For my Life, yes, I'll pay the price if it means prison, "I'll catch up on my reading, and won't have to worry about paying bills." I contemplated ahead of time that they were going to keep me on PC (protective custody) because I worked at the prison, or they would move me to another state so I could be relegated to the general population. I was okay and willing *to go to prison for taking his life* because I was that hurt, that diminished, that trampled upon. Sisters and Brothers, *I want you, NEVER, to reach this point.*

How many times can he humiliate me right into the ground, right in front of people without any care for my feelings or my dignity?? Me, who has been so loving, supportive, and understanding of you—Always. I, who took out a loan for $25,000 to help you with your legal problems because I KNEW not one of those other women who you showered with gifts and money could care less about helping you.

Not one of them gave you a nickel!! I, who gave you another of many chances because I believed you this time; I believed you meant what you said and had grown up.

Today, all the lies and deceit END. -- You are killing me! My self-worth, my dignity, my being, my womanhood. *You have no right to do that.* If no one else will protect me, or defend me, I will do it myself. Sisters and Brothers, you don't want to get to this boiling point: Let me tell you from experience, 'to compensate' for those aching, empty missing gaps in your life—the Year of Lies and Hurts, Chances, Forgiveness, and Understanding, you will fill those holes, more accurately—***pour yourself full of things that temporarily soothe the hurt and pain:*** "Gallons and Gallons of booze, drugs, food, sex, money, relationships—whatever is "Your Drug of Choice."—Whatever it is, it makes you feel good for "the moment," but those moments and days and years ADDICT YOUR ASS, and if you're not careful they will rule you and your entire world for your entire life…until it is no more.

"Addiction – Generational Alcoholism"

My hole and gap-filler happened to be "Seagram's Gin and Lemon Drops." That is what I 'literally' drowned my pain in— nice, cute name for something that nearly killed "All of Me…Body, Mind, Heart, and Soul." When I bought my own house, I thought my life was just going to be complete, like the house came with a husband and kids, and everything I needed to be a family. I didn't take my 'own history' into consideration. I didn't know moving that far away from the family I always lived with, and then becoming a homebody—just working and coming home to an empty place—would have such drastic effects… along with every other abuse and loss.

Then one day it was—"Let me get some gin and lemon," and that's how it started. As simple as that. And I didn't have a problem with it because I was enjoying it; it tasted damn good; it was addictive—who's thinking or caring about that? A nice drink went down real easy but my Grandmother said over and over again, "Bella, why would you drink something that you know killed your sister?" I don't know, once I drank it that night I just decided to drink it again, and again, and again... I got bored and I drank. It was a Tuesday, so then a couple days later, I was like, "Let me get a drink again; let me get some gin and a lemon," till it became a daily thing,—like a job I did for 20 years. I never quit—I'm not a quitter. At Work...or "Drinking."

I never called out and I drank every day...*every single day.* So, what my sister taught me was the 'perfect methodology;' she would cut open the lemon and put salt on it. Then, she would drink the gin straight and then suck on the lemon and that's what you call a "lemon drop." Uh, hold on, we have to think about this financially. I always think from a financially sound perspective... So, now I'm going to buy half a gallon like they have in the restaurant. That is more economical; that will last me for seven days. So, folks, I did that for 20 years. TWENTY YEARS—goes fast, who's counting?

I want to say—2 months before I went into Rehab in 2019—that restaurant-size half gallon of gin (straight) that used to last me 7 days, now lasted me 2 days. The professionals would eventually tell me, they didn't understand how I was living and focusing, having that much alcohol in my system...and to this day, I don't look 51 and especially someone who drank and smoked daily for 20 years! I never went to work drunk and I still had my part-time job that I had for 9 years along with my full-time job.

I was the *Top Model* for the "Functioning Alcoholic." You see, I wasn't thinking of my sister dying because of alcoholism. I just knew if I did it, I was going to make sure that my body was right and healthy. Oh, yeah. My primary doctor said, "I know Dr. Vinay is taking care of you." If I drank the night before, I made sure I would drink 64 ounces of water daily to flush out the gin. I also made sure I walked daily and ate well to help 'inwardly.' I knew I was killing my body so I did as much as possible to stop the bad effects it causes. We had a lab right in the doctor's office where I worked. So, every 4 months I knew it was time to check how my liver was doing.

Being around primary doctors and specialists, I knew what to do to offset "the effects of the alcohol abuse." Many people not having this medical experience, may not know you have to 'flush that stuff out.' Also, "Walk"!! Just don't get drunk, lie down and go to sleep. So, Ms. Bella Smartness made sure I got the proper exercise and ate right. ...How we try and compensate...

I think it was in 2017 when I was working at Lakeland Community Hospital, I had an issue with my arm going numb, and I had to get a cortisone injection in my arm. There was a nerve pain traveling down my arm, and suddenly it just stopped moving. They said it was probably a pinched nerve so they gave me this injection which was supposed to last for 3 months. Two days later, my arm went limp again and I thought I might have had a stroke but it wasn't one. The doctors told me it would be 6 weeks before I could get another injection because of the dye that it puts into your system. I was already on leave from work with short term disability.

I said to myself, "Hey, now that I'm out for 6 weeks, I'll go to Rehab. It's better than sitting around at home drinking; besides I knew my body needed a rest, so I did the 30 days there." However, as soon as I got out, *I drank* because it was the same environment—New Jersey. You see, I can't live in New Jersey—that's like Texas, the death state for me. I'm going to drink as soon as I get there; there's nothing to do—a dead zone. Both of my brothers left New Jersey after Granny died; the youngest brother, Jayden, left first. I went after him, and my brother Brandon soon followed right behind. You can't flourish there. Couple that with your culture, conditioning, and addictions—in our case, Generational Alcoholism: Grandfather, Mother, Father, Brother, Uncles, Aunts, and on and on. Pile on the other abuses and societal pressures, and that becomes a powerful cocktail for you—abysmal self-destruction.

"The Shelter" – Homeless Individuals"

This is the place where I landed with all the cast-out souls of society. Yet, it was these special women who taught me humility, understanding, and compassion at the deepest levels. Many of their life stories were far worse than mine. Many didn't have at least one person they could ever trust or depend upon—certainly no one to instill confidence within themselves. Maybe they were never loved at all. They are not the dregs of society but perhaps the most vulnerable and neglected.

Some are just too fragile. They grew up without any garden—barren dirt from the time they were born—and when confronted with so many catastrophes happening, one after the other, they don't have the sustenance, example, support system to carry the weight, or guide their emotional grief and trauma, so they just walk away. That is the only way they know how "To Survive." No wonder they spend their entire disability checks on booze, food, or drugs. What else do they have to look forward to, to take away the emptiness and pain?

I wish every single one of them the very, very best. It took all of me to lift myself out of that quicksand. At least while I was there, they knew I truly cared; I didn't think I was above or below them so I gained their trust to confide and share their life stories with me. That's what I take with me, a piece of each of them--their lives and inner hearts. There are so many reasons why I was there with them. Maybe I won't discover them until more time passes but I am glad our paths touched if only for a short time.

Many get comfortable there and they don't want to move on, or they don't know how. One lady had been at the same shelter 6 times in her life. 'You need a place to stay, you come; you go away for 6 months a year, get yourself together; and then you fall off and go back again.' The Shelter is always an 'open door,' and unlike jail, you can leave and return as you please, just as long as you follow the rules and are back on time. God Bless Them, at least they have a Home, Shelter, and Food. They truly taught me to "Count My Blessings" and be thankful for each one. They didn't know it but they helped me catapult back into Life...

"Enlightenment and Resolution"

Before your soul is devastated—if I can tell you anything—take stock, see the warning signs, Really Look At Them: Don't Be In DENIAL, Day After Day, Year After Year, it gets tiresome. DON'T GET TO THE POINT WHERE IT'S YOUR LIFE OR THEIRS.

NEWSFLASH – Understanding "Why":

It's got to be more than "damn words"—the Abuser HAS TO "TAKE ACTION"—*Want to Take Action to Get Better.* Each of us has a "free will." Each of us is responsible for our own actions—including staying for a lifetime in a bad situation—when we should have left years before. DOUBLE NEWS FLASH—LISTEN CAREFULLY AND CLOSELY: "YOU CANNOT DO IT FOR THEM." Oh, you've tried: Compassion, understanding, forgiveness—"Oh, poor baby, you didn't have a mother; you grew up with your father beating you; you had no example, da da da." It's true, man! I tried to understand, I tried to give you LOVE to make up for it—MONEY, all that you needed—the only Woman who stuck by you through thick and thin. "I" did not ABANDON YOU. – Your Mother did! WHY ARE YOU BLAMING ME, KICKING ME DOWN FOR YEARS AND YEARS, LYING AND CHEATING, DISRESPECTING <u>ME</u>?? –

(I allowed) "this man" to take so much of my Life: my hopes and dreams, my body, my soul, and my heart—he almost took my Life Force. NEVER LET ANYONE TAKE THAT AWAY FROM YOU. GOD GAVE YOU LIFE, HE'S THE ONLY ONE THAT SHOULD TAKE IT AWAY.

LOVE is the Game-changer—it makes you stay—LIFE is what makes you leave. We are all Human Beings; we all have our breaking points. "GET HELP," before you reach the point of no return as I did- ready to go to jail if the abuser got killed. "You are intelligent. You are a beautiful human being deserving of your Life. We *should be* compassionate, understanding, and forgiving. These are "virtues." But we are not someone's doormat to constantly step on and beat down, or someone's punching bag to take out their aggressions on, or a vulnerable person who is constantly victimized, manipulated, and brutalized.

THERE are 24/7 Resources, from dialing 9-1-1, to victim emergency shelters, and suicide hotlines. We live in a time when we are more culturally evolved to issues of partner and child abuse, molestation, and addiction. Police are more aware, sensitive; and better trained in dealing with these life-altering issues; laws have more power so that they can be enforced. Nothing is yet perfect because we as humans are not perfect. But everything is better than the generations before us, what our grandmothers and grandfathers endured. Men are now being raised by strong independent women, teaching them to be "Men," *Gentle*men, and not abusers. We are all learning that *every minute, every day of our lives, and all our time on Earth is precious.*

FIND WHAT'S ROTTING YOUR SOUL, FACE IT LIKE THE DEMON IT IS, AND LEAVE FOR ANOTHER WHERE YOU CAN PLANT YOUR OWN GARDEN. TAKE STOCK OF WHAT WAS GOOD, REMEMBER IT AND MOVE ON. We have so many more resources today than women and men had before us. – Hey, I'm aware Men also are being abused, shot, killed, and manipulated!– ABUSE knows no gender, racial ethnicity, class, age, education, state or country.

- You can't bury what's hurting you, it will just decay inside and poison you.
- You can't pretend it's not there; it will *ghost* you day and night.
- You can't heal it by pouring things in the missing holes that will surely become addictions.
- You must dig it out, face it, mourn what you didn't have, and move on to celebrate Life and Freedom.

Be aware of ALL your "resources;" they may Save your Life, so keep them near and use them. Nothing is perfect, but at least you'll fight for your life, and your children's lives, informed and armored, not with guns but with intelligence, information, and resources. The "signs" are always there; friends, take off the *shades* and get to know your soul.

IF YOU'RE GONNA DIE, YOU'RE GONNA DIE TRYING "TO LIVE." - Was that my Granny speaking to me? I think so... She knew I was hard-headed. She knew sometimes I was too kind for my own good; she knew she had given me all she could...but she had faith I would find my own way if it were from the darkest, deepest place. When I told my Granny when she was dying, I wouldn't make it without her. She told me, "Bella, you're stronger than you think." She had faith in me. But the key that unlocked the door was, "I" had to have faith in me, and truly find myself.

A "good therapist," one that *you're comfortable with and can relate to*, can help you navigate those muddy waters. Today, many professional counselors work on sliding scales and are available to everyone, including the homeless. We are just too close to our own selves and predicaments. We need a neutral person who is trained professionally so they can be observers and help us discover how we continuously self-sabotage ourselves, how we are manipulated or are the manipulators, help us uncover the wounds we are unable to witness without someone who can help us do it. It isn't easy.... I'm still looking for that compatible therapist *"for me."* But I know I will find that person because I want to. The energy, the prayer I send out is: *I want to get better. I want to find the means and God, the Universe, and positive energy will bring it forth.*

Gone are the days when the mentality was, "If he/she would just change..." Each of us has a free will. It is their choice if they want to change or not. One of the hardest truisms is "Respect their decisions, value your own, and move on." And if they won't let you, go to ALL your Resources and Protection, and your Professional Advisor to help support and guide you. DON'T GIVE UP. – You Are Worth It! Is there anything more important than YOU or YOUR LIFE? NO.

YOU ARE NOT ALONE. I Love You, and I don't even know you, *but* I know what you are going through...what you have been through. ALL the people that have gone through/are going through what you did stand with you. Compassionate, God said we must be. - I can have compassion for you, but I can't help you until you truly want to help yourself. I cannot or will not be someone's doormat or punching bag. I'm sorry you were hurt in your childhood, but I personally didn't do it, don't beat a woman or a man because your mother or father beat and abandoned you, and don't beat up yourself, because YOU did nothing. I Love You, but I have learned your Life begins—when you learn to Love Yourself.

I'm here for you, Cheering You on!

Love
Bella

Chapter 13

"How Does My Garden Grow?" "HOME"

If my "Family Tree" has broken or missing limbs, I'd rather cut them off completely and grow my own tree, even if it doesn't come directly from my DNA or branches.

-Weed out those old ghosts and goblins so they are not shadowing your life, forever keeping the sunshine away to prevent growth, sticking to you like residue in your life you haven't been able to wash off. Be brutally honest with yourself. Are you keeping dead memory souvenirs out of sentimentality or people in your life because *'you are enabling them,'* or have they become *'addictions'?'* All the dead weight may be preventing many new flowers from blossoming and many new people from coming into your heart and life. A whole new garden is waiting to grow! -Do you need to start from scratch? Find new soil, plant yourself in a new town or city, a different climate, a different country, where you can start new in a totally new environment.

-A seed doesn't stay quivering in the ground, and it is not afraid to grow. If given the proper care, attention, and nourishment, identifying its needs and what it doesn't need—not giving it too much or too little—it grows! It is "natural to grow" and unnatural to stop or stunt our growth. Is your soul trying to speak, to live, to breathe, and someone or something is suffocating it? "Break through," and reach out for the resources waiting to help you.

-Find the holes and gaps in you and your life. Do you need more nitrogen in the soil, more plant food, more sunlight, more water, and more supplements because you are depleted in something and need to be nourished and strengthened? Are you 'exercising life,' or becoming lifeless and letting it pass you by? What is missing in your life? – Take stock of your Garden!

- Are you compensating for what is missing by filling yourself full of food, alcohol, drugs, and addictions? Pouring gallons of alcohol down your throat, filling your body with poison, and self-medicating yourself with the wrong things or people is only temporary, and it takes control of your ass. IT WANTS ALL OF YOU—your mind, heart, body, and spirit Stand tall, face your demons, and slay the mother fuckers. "You Are Stronger than You Know! You are not alone; all the Sisters and Brothers who have made the journey "out" are right next to you, even though you can't see them.

Remember, this is not just anyone's Garden. **This is Your Garden**, with your own Needs and your own Wishes. You can tailor it just for you. No one needs to see it but you—your "secret garden" within.

-It's you who tends to it; it is you who is the Gardener of your own soul. If something's not growing or taking to the soil, you can change it, root it up, and start again.

-Ask for help and keep at it until you find the right professional you can trust, one that is giving you the help you need and ask for, one that is helping you find your true self that has been dying to come out.

-In your Garden, plant a beautiful seed right in the center; call it—Self-Love; "Love Thyself." Women are fixers; we have to learn to 'fix ourselves' and 'love ourselves' first before we can learn to love another. If we don't think we are worthy of love, then why would anyone else want to love us? The same applies to men. Self-sabotage: we often see it in others, and perhaps we need to turn the mirror within and really look at what and who is staring back at us. Be happy and proud of that image, and if it needs fixing or nurturing, "Self-Care and Self-Love.".

- And if you have no "Granny" or special person like that in your life, plant that special 'rose' that will become one. *"To Love Yourself is the Key to Your Home."* My special rose appeared just after my 51st birthday; her name is Elle, and I think I was "growing her" inside with hope and belief and God's inspiration, and she appeared just when I needed her...and probably when I was ready for her—"Grown-up and Healing"—a different person now and wanting a different kind of person in my life. God said, *"Ask and it will be given to you; seek and you will find; knock and the door will be opened to you."*

-And if there is 'no growth?' ...Why not? What kind of seeds are you planting? Maybe more positive, healing seeds are needed? What is preventing the seeds you plant from growing?

-Are you nourishing the seeds and yourself properly and daily, and with the right thoughts and actions? Surrounding yourself with positive, happy people? A clean, healthy environment? Trying different things, falling down, and getting back up is how we learn. Making the same mistake over and over again keeps us in a damn hole we just keep digging ourselves out of.

-Each of us has that seed of courage in our soil's DNA. We just need to nurture it, encourage it, protect it, and keep it alive and strong (when others try to destroy it). It will grow branches of self-esteem and self-confidence and make you strong and courageous. Look for your new leaves and congratulate yourself.

-We must become the proud Gardeners of our own "Secret Garden." Think of it as a secret bank account of tenacity, stamina, willpower, resolution, and bravery that will grow into our own empowerment when we need it the most.

As tall as the tree is, so are its roots wide. How long has your generational tree been feeding on the wrong ideas and behaviors—perpetuating the wrong values, being uncared for, feeding machoism, victimization, abandonment, and brutality? It was my Granny, the solid, wise, forward-thinking Gardener, who walked right into the middle of the land and planted a new tree trunk, a new "Family Tree." She planted new energy and seeds into her Family Garden because she was different. She brought new ways of thinking and grew her branches with Love and Strength, all powered by God. And she knew her granddaughter would use one of the new roots to create her own tree and plant her own garden.

My Granny left behind that soil in which were deeply buried the generational ideas and renourished her garden with belief in God and to treat every fellow person with respect, the way you wished to be treated. She traveled the world so she could see new things and observe new kinds of people and terrain, and she brought that back to our Family garden. And now that she's nurtured the soil and strengthened its roots, I can start my own garden. It will have all the high-quality plants of character and moral integrity that Granny cultivated her entire life within each of us, her class and dignity, her light and wisdom, and her moral strength of character that will flourish in her granddaughter Bella's Garden. Following Granny's lead, I didn't just try to "bury the old." I dug up the whole damn mess and chucked every single shred of it. But I am building again—stronger and more beautiful and plentiful than ever before. It will be a garden that Granny would be proud of—the newness, the individuality, the hope, and the courage. Branches will grow strong and bear new fruit and flowers.

We have to become the proud Gardener of our own "Secret Garden." Remember, it's your own secret account where we grow and store our stamina, courage, determination, and perseverance so it can grow with interest every day without anyone's knowledge, and when we need it the most, it will be the source of great empowerment that enables us to be "Free." We are never free when someone is abusing our body and strangling our soul.

Funky Dineva said something like, "Please learn to love yourself and know your worth." And I'll add, "I saw your face in Rehab, in The Shelter, in the Prisons, at the Office, on the Street, and I am here with you. I know what you have/are going through. I am here to support and encourage you every step of the way. I Love You. Now, it is time for *You* to "Love You."

"Home"
Healing is a process

The journey to find "Home" is a process; for some, it may take a lifetime. But the sooner you make up your mind to take the first step, the sooner you begin the process. Whenever that day, that moment, that year comes, remember, "You can't peel off all the layers at once; you'd die—you'd be butt naked, and down to your blood and bones. Just remember how many years, layers, and depths you have accumulated until you reach this point.

With me, you saw the journey from Granny's beautiful garden to finding my mother on the ground bloody from drugs and a suicide attempt when I was 5, to finding out there was no support from the two people who brought you into the world and you could never receive the most important thing you needed from them—"LOVE," to falling in love with an abuser—physically, mentally, emotionally, and spiritually—who I tried to 'over-love' by compensating for the love and support he never had. He, too, would never be able to give me what I needed most—Love and Respect.

And then the downward spiral of my life began—attempting suicide because I lost my dream—a husband (through abuse), children (through a hysterectomy), a house that I had built at 25 and lost.

...And to fill "All the Gaps and Deep Holes," for 20 years, I drowned myself in alcohol—enough to fill a trainload of fuel tankers—and, finally, the spiral ended when, having lost it all, I fell into the bottomless pit of hell in a "Shelter" because I had given everything up, including my family. The irony was it was here I found "HOME," in a homeless shelter where other women just like me found themselves *'without a home.'*

LOVE is the "Gamechanger." I think we want and need it more than anything else in Life. We will almost kill ourselves to get it... but I think finding Love starts at home. I found that "Home" is not a place or a building, even if you build it yourself from the ground up, even if it costs a billion dollars, and even if you can pay that exorbitant amount. Home is the deepest place inside of yourself, where you reside—the truest, purest, most innocent part of you that God made—it just may take the better part of a lifetime to find it and uncover it—since the day you are born, all else attempts to cover it, abuse it, and make it over.

But if the sharing of my life, my abuse, family dysfunction, alcoholic addiction, loss of "everything," *and* how I survived can help you learn from my life, my challenges, my errors, and my fears, then all the pain endured is worth it. One Life is worth "Everything," and it will be my privilege to help you, encourage you, and support you in your own Journey to Live and find your own "HOME." There is nothing in the world like that peace and sanctuary when you discover the real "YOU." Don't let anyone take that away from you. Don't ever get to the point where it's your life or theirs. Hope, Support, and Professional Friends are all around you today. Grab them with both hands. If you die trying, at least you fought for life... with all the tools you had.

The real meaning of Home is to find your true self. I found that even in building my own house, furnishing it with pretty things, and putting a "Man" and Children inside it, it can be just 4 walls with cardboard figures that you have placed within it. – This is what society said everyone should have and work their whole life for— "This is what will make you happy." Not if you don't know who you are and what you really want. Look at my Life. I'm not with a man; I'm with Elle a beautiful woman. …And maybe it wasn't meant for me to have children. Maybe God is steering me toward a new dream. This is Life. What if—you can still be the most whole person you can be—even though you don't have a mother, father, husband, or mate? "Home is You" and what you make of it. Find yourself, and you will find the real Home that resides within you.

Wishing you Success and Blessings
on Your Journey HOME:
"Welcome Home!"

Love,
Bella

Resources Page

Help is Available

-The Trevor Project:

A national organization that offers crisis intervention and suicide prevention services to LGBTQ+ young people ages 13–24.

24/7 crisis services lifeline is available at (866) 488-7386.

-LGBT National Hotline: Offers free and confidential peer support, information, and local resources.

(888) 843-4564.

-LGBT National Coming Out Support Hotline:

(800) 246-7743.

-211:

This hotline connects people in most areas of the United States to local social services and emergency housing referrals.

-National Runaway Safeline:

This hotline offers free, confidential, and non-judgmental support 24 hours a day by calling:

1-800-RUNAWAY (1-800-786-2929). People can also text, live chat, or email an agent for help.

-National Sexual Assault Hotline:

Hours Available 24 hours

800-646-4673

-Mental Health Hotline

Hours Available 24 hours

Call 866-903-3787

Text 866-903-3787

Chat 866-903-3787

-988 Suicide and Crisis Lifetime:

Languages English and Spanish

Hours Available 24 hours

Call 988

Text 988

Chat 988

-National Domestic Violence Hotline:

Languages: English, Spanish and 200+ through interpretation service

Hours: 24/7

Call 800-799-7233

Text BEGIN to 88788

-SAMHSA's National Helpline: a confidential, free, 24-hour-a-day, 365-day-a-year, information service, in English and Spanish, for individuals and family members facing mental and/or substance use disorders. This service provides referrals to local treatment facilities, support groups, and community-based organization

1-800-662-HELP (4357) (also known as the Treatment Referral Routing Service), or TTY: 1-800-487-4889 is

Author Bios

Bella St. Patrick, Co-author

Bella St. Patrick is a survivor of physical, mental, and sexual abuse. This is the first novel she decided to write not only for therapy purposes but in the hopes that she will give strength to others who have been harmed. She also hopes to stop anyone from making the many mistakes she has made in life, and that in itself would be an accomplishment she will relish. She is also a proud member of the LBGTQIA + community. In her professional life, Bella has a diversity of job experiences: in the military, as a Corrections Officer in a state prison, as a Medical Front Office Coordinator for Physicians and Cardiologists, and as a Caretaker for a wonderful young man who was born blind, autistic, and had cerebral palsy. From whatever job she encounters, Bella takes a wealth of experience from it. She feels every human being she has contact with enriches her life.

In her travels, she has witnessed one thing over and over. It is very true in what they say there is only 6 degrees of separation. She has been around people from all walks of life: the affluent to the middle class, and even the poorest of the poor, and what she has found is they all have the same thing in common. They all want to be loved, heard, and respected.

A special thank you goes out to Funky Dineva: "Funky Dineva, I express my gratitude and admiration to YOU. I watched you for years on your YouTube channel bare your soul with the good, the bad, and the ugly of your life. You have helped me through 2 marriages, 2 divorces, rehab, and homelessness. I remember on my bad days—and there were many—how you would turn my tears into hysterical laughter when I heard those words "QUIET AS ITS KEPT" 'cuz I knew it was going to be some mess. Lol. And as you always say, "NEVER LET A BITCH SPRAY YOU WITH YOUR OWN TEA."

Thank you for inspiring me to tell my story with the courage, dignity, and respect I give to you for telling your life story."

Thank you for reading my book. I hope you enjoy...

Bella St. Patrick

Arista, Co-author

Arista is an award-winning author/actor living in New York City. Her stage plays, *All About Sneakers* and *Welcome Home Kelly!*, have had Off-Broadway productions. Her screenplay *USA* heralds the "1st Homeless Street Soccer World Cup" in Graz, Austria; her screen and stage play, *What Would the Founding Fathers Tell Us Today,* adapted from Werner Neff's book, remind us who built the foundation of America and what our forebearers would say today. Her memoir book, *CHAD, A Celebration of Life – Beyond a Mother's Memories,* recounts her son's 26 years on earth and the many lives he touched, his own cut short by Sudden Cardiac Death in Young Athletes. His nonprofit organization, "The Chad Foundation for Athletes and Artists," has safeguarded 10,000 young hearts with echocardiogram screenings and is supported by Adam Silver, the Commissioner of the NBA. She is honored to co-author with Elle Louise in her real-life story, *'TIL TIMES GET BETTER,* and bring 'to life' her voyage of years of devastating child abuse and her escape to become a "Survivor." Recently, she is proud to co-author with Bella St. Patrick in her life story *BROKEN BUT HEALING*, hailing her triumphs in buying her own home at 25, surviving devastating abuse and addiction spiraling to homelessness at 50, and her indomitable, victorious quest back to life. Arista hopes these books will be inspirational healing tools for those experiencing abuse and addiction. Her most significant role is mother to her 3 sons, Chad, Curt, and Collin, and a dedication to the gift of safeguarding Hearts and creating Art that uplifts the Human Spirit. www.chad-foundation.org

Printed in the United States
by Baker & Taylor Publisher Services